TAROT
FOR **TODAY**

TAROT
FOR **TODAY**

Joanna Watters

CARROLL & BROWN PUBLISHERS LIMITED

For Sue, my twin sister.
For a lifetime of love and belief.

First published in the UK in 2003 by
CARROLL & BROWN PUBLISHERS LIMITED
20 Lonsdale Road, Queen's Park,
London, NW6 6RD

Project Editor Michelle Bernard
Art Editor Gilda Pacitti

A CIP catalogue record for this book is available
from the British Library

ISBN 1-903258-57-X
Reproduced by RALI, Spain
Printed by Tien Wah Press, Singapore
First Edition

CONTENTS

INTRODUCTION

The Tarot is growing rapidly in popularity, indicated by its increased presence in the popular press alongside Sun signs and horoscopes. This growth can also be seen as a reflection of people's need and search for meaning in their lives.

The Tarot is widely misunderstood. All too often it is written off either as foolishness or nonsense, along with other popular forms of divination such as astrology and palmistry. It is seen as only for the weak-minded or the gullible, for those who blindly "believe in" such things. Furthermore, in many people's minds, the Tarot is associated with clairvoyance, or the occult. It belongs only to those who already possess psychic ability or second sight, or it is simply "spooky," shrouded in taboo and superstition, and grouped along with seances and ouija boards.

In this respect the Tarot is in a different camp from astrology which, even though it has been kept alive largely through the predictive format of Sun sign columns and phonelines, is more likely to be regarded as a craft as opposed to a psychic gift. This book aims to show that the Tarot has its own special brand of magic but is also a craft, an acquired skill that anyone can learn. To illustrate this point, Chapter One deals with the difference between clairvoyance and divination and explores the nature of symbolism. Only with an understanding of these points can we address the basis of common misconceptions about the Tarot.

Tarot now takes its place alongside popular astrology in magazines and newspapers, a clear indication of its revival and growing popularity. This also reflects the need for meaning in modern life. As we move into the new millennium, there is an ever-increasing focus on achievement, materialism, and rapidly developing

A modern approach to the Tarot

You will find that there are many publications available that look at the history of the Tarot and how the cards and their meanings have evolved over the years. While this is interesting, an academic approach is not essential when it comes to understanding the Tarot, either from the reader's or the client's point of view. From my own long and varied experience of doing readings, I have found there to be little interest in the history of divinatory practices. Clients are concerned only with the content of their own readings, how the cards can reflect their personal situations and relationships, and the accuracy or value of predictions or guidance. Therefore, it is not within the scope of this book to examine the history of the Tarot cards, but to update their value, purpose, and meaning in a modern context through a "hands-on" approach.

technology. Never has the scientific attitude been so predominant but, inevitably, this brings its own reaction and more and more people are now struggling to reclaim a spiritual dimension, a deeper connection with their inner world.

THE TAROT DECK

There is currently an enormous variety of Tarot packs on the market, but there are no hard and fast rules as to the relative merits of each one. The best rule to follow is personal preference, so choose the deck whose pictures and images most appeal to you. The easier it is to familiarize yourself with your cards, the easier it will be for you to work with them.

I originally learned the Tarot with the well-known Rider-Waite pack, devised by A.E. Waite and illustrated by Pamela Colman Smith. The vision and understanding behind this collaboration is reflected in the simple but powerful images in the pack, which lead us easily into their symbolic meaning. The pack used in this book is the Universal Waite, which is based on the Rider-Waite. Whichever deck you use, it will consist of 78 cards that form three categories—the Major Arcana, the Minor Arcana, and the Court Cards.

There are many different versions of the Tarot deck. The one shown here is the Universal Waite.

The Major Arcana These consist of 22 cards, from the Fool, numbered 0, through to the World, numbered 21. These are arguably the most important cards of the deck, as they embody archetypes and are rich with psychological associations. Astrological symbolism carries the same weight and complexity, so I have matched each of the Major Arcana cards with an astrological counterpart. Even if you are not a student of astrology, you will, hopefully, find these comparisons helpful when learning the meaning of the cards and bringing their symbolism and meaning to life.

The Minor Arcana These consist of four suits with ten cards in each, from the Ace through to the Ten. These 40 cards can add a great deal of information, depth, and detail to a reading. The Wands, Pentacles, Swords, and Cups correlate to the four elements of Fire, Earth, Air, and Water. Astrology assigns particular qualities and characteristics to each element, and these are listed at the beginning of each section. Again, these correlations are given in order to enhance and flesh out the meaning of these cards.

The Court Cards These comprise of the remaining 16 cards—a Page, a Knight, a King, and a Queen for each of the four suits. Often these cards speak of other people in our lives, so I have listed the zodiac signs that correspond to each element, as this link can help to illustrate

Correlations between the Tarot cards and astrological signs can help to enhance the meaning of the cards.

the type of personality in question. I have also assigned one or more of the planets to each group, such as Venus for the Queens and Mars for the Knights.

THE ROLE OF THE READER

The role of the Tarot reader is threefold. He or she is diviner, interpreter, and counselor, and how to learn and combine these skills is a theme that runs throughout the book.

As Diviner The Tarot reader takes up the more traditional role of the one who "sees" the future, the one who makes pronouncements and judgements. But today's Tarot reader is more than just a fortune-teller whose predictions announce tall, dark strangers and wins on the lottery. The route to divination is more sophisticated than the stereotypical clairvoyant world of tea leaves and crystal balls would suggest. In modern practice predictions actually constitute a relatively small part of a reading, and they are the closing statement rather than the opening speech. You may be surprised to learn that some readings do not require any predictive content at all.

As Interpreter The Tarot reader communicates the symbolic language of the Tarot, explaining and framing the client's individual situation within the images presented by the cards in a spread. And while it would be a mistake to try and "teach" your craft as you work, I always try to invite my client into the world of symbolism as quickly as possible. From the example readings in chapters two, three, and four, you will see that I generally start this process by describing the card pictorially, and the immediacy of the Tarot in this respect is enormously helpful.

Illustrating how the cards mirror and amplify our lives helps the client to adopt the "symbolic attitude." In other words, the reading will only make sense if it is placed within the all important framework of context, allowing the client to see how symbolism works and how the reading offers symbolism pertinent to him or her. For this reason, I have given as many examples as possible from my own readings, letting each anecdote illustrate individual cards, showing how a card can come to life and speak volumes when it forms a meaningful link in the chain of a story. Only by seeing symbolism in action is the true magic of divination revealed to us.

As Counselor Today's Tarot reader must also be able to wear the therapist's hat. When I first started practicing astrology, I soon realized that clients did not come because they wanted me to calculate their Ascendant or to find out about their Moon sign. They came because they were looking for guidance or answers and, as an astrologer, I was expected not only to provide these answers but also to talk about and understand their problems. The same principle applies to the Tarot, so we must always guard against over-explaining the cards at the expense of uncovering the real, important issues.

You will always get clients who say they are "just interested," and that may or may not be true, but nine times out of ten, people will seek you out because they are wrestling with a problem that is causing stress, pain, anxiety, or confusion. This means that, as practicing Tarot readers, we are dealing with the delicate fabric of other people's lives, and it is vital that we acquire some basic counseling skills. We cannot expect to become expert therapists overnight, and skills in this department can be honed only with time and experience. However, we can be aware of the basic principles, so chapter five is designed to offer insights and guidelines regarding the emotional and psychological considerations of doing readings. Chapter six is devoted to the practical skills involved in conducting a reading, with examples of spreads that are easy to learn and use from the outset.

Throughout the book I have tried to keep in mind the reader who is completely new to the world of divination. At the same time, I hope that the more advanced student will find the material presented useful and informative. I have aimed to address the kinds of questions that I have been asked over the years by students and clients, and have tried as much as possible to convert theory into practice. As with any subject, we can never stop learning, so this book is by no means a definitive manual. While I hope it will engage your interest and add to your knowledge, my main wish is that it will encourage and inspire you in your own studies and development as a sensitive Tarot reader.

Even if the client has never laid eyes on a Tarot card before, he or she will quickly connect with the images, such as Swords for strife or Cups for love.

There is a vital link between divination and symbolism, and understanding this link changes our perception of what it means to be a Tarot reader or astrologer. These arcane crafts are not rooted in clairvoyance but in the intuitive and creative skills that we all possess. This chapter introduces astrology and demonstrates how to use it in a Tarot reading without having to calculate a horoscope.

1

DIVINATION VERSUS CLAIRVOYANCE

DIVINATION VERSUS CLAIRVOYANCE

Whether you treat the Tarot as an outside interest or as your full-time profession, you will, inevitably, encounter an enormous variety of reactions to it from other people.

Even now, with 15 years' experience behind me, I still tense slightly when someone asks me what I do. This is because I know there will be an immediate response, but that it won't necessarily be one of keen interest. Many people find the Tarot fascinating, but in that initial moment of inquiry, I know that I am just as likely to pick up on scorn, embarrassment, amusement, or even anger.

There is a lot of prejudice, but it is important to remember that such reactions are products of fear or ignorance. This is partly due to the powerful role of the media, which is a double-edged sword for the professional world of divination. While newspapers and magazines keep the Tarot in the public eye, they also mostly present just the predictive, one-dimensional face that can never be taken seriously. Few people stop to wonder if there is more to the Tarot than a three-card reading, which is presented as predicting a definite future, no matter what your question or personal situation may be.

It does not take much investigation to discover that random judgements from the Tarot at the end of a phone line bear little or no relation to the art of working on a full spread with an individual client. The fortune-teller image has been difficult to scotch and the stereotypical picture of tarot readers is still alive and kicking—

someone sitting under a star-studded canopy, wearing a headscarf and sporting huge earrings, with a strange name, who is in some way odd, scary, ridiculous, out of touch with reality, or even mad.

YOU DON'T REALLY BELIEVE IN ALL OF THIS, DO YOU?

I have lost count of how many times I have been asked this question and I used to detest it. It is a question that usually drips with ridicule, but it is in fact perfect for taking on the debate simply because divination is not about *belief* but about *knowing*. Questions of belief are questions of faith, such as, "Do you believe in God?" This stance implies that the Tarot reader is merely being impelled by his or her own belief system, which may even amount to a kind of blindness. He or she is seen to be motivated by an insistence on something that cannot be proved, "believing in" something simply because of the desire for it to be true.

In answer to this question from a man who worked on a flotilla, I pointed to the seafront and asked him, "Do you believe that yacht can sail? Of course you do, because you know it can sail. You've seen it happen hundreds of times." When the Tarot reader sees that a spread works, he or she moves into the position of knowing rather than believing. When you have seen spreads work hundreds of times, that knowledge becomes your security, the

Many celebrities are well-known for visiting Tarot readers, including the late Princess Diana, who regularly consulted a Tarot reader based in London.

Divination and clairvoyance

Clairvoyance is derived from the French for "clear" and "sight," but it has come to mean more than keen-sightedness. If we say someone is clairvoyant, we mean that they are psychic, which generally means that this person has some kind of natural second sight. They have not necessarily developed their psychic skills consciously. They simply see, hear, or know things without being told or without being asked. This is the realm of *unbidden* information or omens.

Divination is derived from the Latin *divinare*, which means to foretell or predict. The modern definition is "the foretelling of future events or discovery of what is hidden or obscure by supernatural or magical means." [1] The essential difference, then, is that divination is an act of consultation, through the means of the Tarot cards, astrology, palmistry, oracles, etc. This is the realm of *bidden* information or omens.

bedrock of your confidence. When that confidence really roots itself, you will notice the difference in your work. You will become sure-footed instead of stumbling.

Knowing how to interpret a Tarot spread is not the result of psychic abilities but the result of learning—the acquisition of certain skills. Some of these skills are due to knowledge, from learning the traditional meanings of the cards, while others are due to your intuitive and creative talents, learning how to think symbolically and how to interpret a symbol within a specific context. As with any other craft, the degree of success depends initially on the amount of time and effort invested, and then on subsequent learning and experience.

Natural talent inevitably comes into play and you may find that you are simply "good at" symbolism. You may also find, as you progress, that you develop your own psychic abilities. You may experience this as heightened intuition, such as picking up on a thread of thought and pulling it

through, or going along with a sense of conviction that may seem totally unrelated to the cards on the table. You may find that a certain word is buzzing in your head, demanding to be spoken. You may also get a strong physical reaction, such as butterflies or a tightening in your stomach, or a headache. If this happens to me it is usually with someone in distress who needs a lot of empathy. The important thing is to pay close attention to any feelings that arise in the course of a reading, as they are telling you something. And the more receptive you are, the stronger the dynamic connection between you, the cards, and your client will be.

THE **NATURE** OF **SYMBOLISM**

It is almost impossible to enter into the world of the symbolic without reference to Carl Jung, who practically invented it. It is from him that we find the best definition of symbolism.

Jung makes his definition of symbolism by comparing a symbol to a sign:

"The sign is always less than the concept it represents, while a symbol always stands for something more than its obvious and immediate meaning." [2]

In other words, a symbol is full of meaning and rich with possibilities. It cannot stand for just one known thing because it would then be merely a name. A sign advertises itself, is obvious and self-explanatory, whereas a symbol is obscure and its meaning has to be teased out.

However, to say that a symbol is full of many possible meanings is very different from saying that anything goes. Understanding this principle is crucial to the foundation of interpretation.

THE WORLD OF DREAMS

To enter the world of symbolism, what better place to start than our dream world? As our conscious mind sleeps, the unconscious wakes up and speaks to us in the pictorial language of images—symbols that do not mean anything until they are questioned. If you have ever offered up a dream for analysis to a friend, a therapist, or yourself, you will know when an interpretation is "right" and "true." You may ponder various interpretations, but when the right one comes up, it has the

A tiger under the bed

A client who came for a reading about her marriage reported a dream in which a tiger was crouching and growling under the bed, getting ready to spring. In the dream she knew that it needed feeding or it would attack her. With the geographical context of the bedroom it didn't take much inquiry to establish that her husband was a "real tiger" in bed and that they had always had a good sex life—until recently. Her sexual withdrawal from him was rooted in anger, and she could see how the tiger symbolized this as well as her husband's frustration. A crucial factor in dream analysis is the feelings evoked and the main feeling in her dream was fear. The fact that she was frightened of the tiger struck at the true heart of her biggest issue—that she was actually frightened of her husband and sick of being prey to his explosive temper, a truth that she was only just beginning to admit to herself.

unmistakable ring of truth about it, and you are impressed. A message from the unconscious has got through, and these messages connect us with insights that may otherwise have passed us by.

As with the Tarot, dreams require context for accurate interpretation. There is the manifest content—what the dream appears to be about on the surface, and the latent content—the hidden or obscure symbolic meaning that needs to be uncovered. Jung's words encapsulate this point perfectly:

"...I have always said to my pupils: 'Learn as much as you can about symbolism; then forget it all when you are analyzing a dream.' This advice is of such practical importance that I have made it a rule to remind myself that I can never understand somebody else's dream well enough to interpret it correctly." [3]

In the woman's dream (see box left), the manifest content is the tiger under the bed and her fear of it. The latent content is what the tiger means to her, who or what it symbolizes, and how it could be interpreted within the context of her life. Someone else could dream about a tiger and it would mean something entirely different. This is why books purporting to analyze dreams never really work, and why learning predetermined meanings for symbols doesn't work either. In fact, nothing kills an attempt at interpretation faster than deciding what a symbol means in advance and without context.

When we are asleep, our unconscious communicates to us through images— symbols that contain hidden meanings or insights for us.

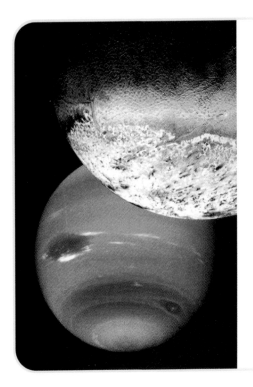

Astrological symbolism

Anyone who has struggled with astrological symbolism will identify with the dilemma over whether to use predetermined meanings or interpret within context. We all start by learning about the signs of the zodiac and then about the combination of signs with planets. We learn that planets are in dignity (strong) in certain signs and in detriment (weak) in others. We learn about the houses, the division of the horoscope into 12 sections, and we then attempt to combine the meanings of a certain planet, in a certain sign, in a certain house.

It is at this point that we realize that there is no magical formula for interpretation because the same combinations can mean different things in different horoscopes. In the words of astrologer Maggie Hyde, "the symbol's meaning continually eludes definition and vexes intellect by being no one thing." [4]

INTERPRETING THE TAROT

The same variety of interpretation applies to learning the symbolism of the Tarot. The more we try to box and categorize symbolism, the more it refuses to play—it becomes flat, lifeless, and mute. Like Jung's pupils, we have to come to grips with the paradox of learning keywords and then forgetting them, or at least not allowing ourselves to be constrained by them. In the name of accurate interpretation we must always remind ourselves that presuppositions tend to cloud and obscure rather than clarify, and if we cling to keywords, we can all too easily end up in a symbolic straitjacket. So where does this leave us?

We can never lose sight of the fact that symbolism is essentially fluid, lively, and dynamic, but our most important frame of reference is the bigger picture, which acts as a faithful guide. In other words, none of the cards will ever mean just one thing, but they will always speak of matters relating to their own dominion. So we can learn manifest meanings while remaining open-minded to the infinite possibilities of the latent meanings.

For example, the Minor Arcana consists of four suits, each of which represents particular aspects and facets of personalities or situations. The Cups, for instance, speak of love, relationships, and our emotional lives, and each of the cards in this suit has its own story to tell, such as the Two for togetherness and union, the Three for celebration, the Four for despondency, and so on. These surface meanings provide a framework for a reading, but it is only when the reading is under way and a card is seen in context that the finer details will emerge.

The same applies to the Major Arcana cards. Let's take the Death card as an example. The Death card speaks of endings or loss and the consequent need for change and adjustment, often in a way that is painful or extremely challenging. If you turn to the anecdote given for this card (card 13, page 57), you will see that I recount a reading in which the Death card spoke of a bereavement, but it was actually the impact of the bereavement that encapsulated the meaning of the card for the client.

In another reading for a woman in her mid-forties, the Death card came up as the center card of the Celtic Cross. The center card can be read as "the heart of the matter," the card that speaks of where we are right now. Before I could say a word, she put her finger on the card and said, "That's how I feel. Dead." The ensuing tale was one of depression, guilt, isolation, and plain boredom. Trapped in her own private hell, she could see no way out. There were, in fact, several ways out, but she was only just beginning to recognize this. The Death card was incredibly powerful for her, as the card spoke to her in a way that moved her, making her see that she was too young to "die" or to offer up her own life as a sacrifice to others.

For another woman asking about the future of a relationship, the Death card showed as the outcome. This did not mean that he or she would die, but that the relationship would. She admitted that it was already dying on its feet and that, in her heart of hearts, she knew that it had been a mistake from the beginning. He was another wrong choice in a series of doomed love affairs and the Death card reinforced the message that she needed to

Boiling over

When you are engaged in a reading, the whole experience can be much easier and more effective if your client already has an awareness of the symbolic. I remember doing a reading for a woman whose relationship was in a mess, and arguments, hurt feelings, hot tempers, and tears had become almost daily events. During our conversation she told me that the boiler in her house had blown up that morning. The symbolist in me immediately leapt to the symbolic connection of the element of water with emotions and their "blowing up" at each other, with steam coming out of their ears.

I offered this interpretation and added, as I always do, that this way of looking at the world may seem strange at first but that it could prove useful to her. She smiled, aware of the humorous connection, but I could tell that she still considered it to be an unrelated event, something annoying happening "to" them at the worst possible moment. She saw no other connection, but as a symbolist you stop believing in coincidences and start believing in synchronicity. Their problems were at boiling point, the relationship had overheated and needed to be cooled down. While I could hold this insight of the relationship needing a thermostat, and use it to assist my own understanding, the reading would probably have been more powerful for her had she tapped into the idea of stress and inner conflict manifesting in her outer world.

The Death card can sometimes indicate that a relationship is dying or has already come to an end.

In other words, if you do not acknowledge the importance of the symbolic, then the act of interpretation becomes pointless. A dream may be remembered only for its manifest content, while the latent content lies dormant and the opportunity for understanding and development slips away unnoticed. Going back to my client's dream about the tiger, she could have woken from the dream, shuddered at it, and attached no further significance to it. However, she was acutely aware of the unhealthy state of her marriage, and the symbolism of the dream constituted a powerful message, bridging the gap between her conscious and unconscious fears, and urging her toward movement, change, and self-protection.

stop and look at why she was attracting "dead-end" relationships.

From these examples, we can see how the Death card fulfills its symbolic role even though the stories are very different. It is also important to note how the card spoke to each person in a powerful and pertinent way. In the other example readings throughout this book, you will see that the symbolic attitude is crucial to the effectiveness of any reading.

THE SYMBOLIC ATTITUDE

Jung defines symbolism for us in the objective sense but he puts equal weight on the subjective factor in play. He states that for something to be a symbol depends on the attitude of the person perceiving it:

"It is obvious that if you assume the dream to be symbolic, you will interpret it differently from a person who believes that the essential energizing thought or emotion is known already and is merely 'disguised' by the dream." [5]

FATE OR FREE WILL?

This has got to be the $64,000 question— the ultimate debate about the nature of the human condition, tackled by the great thinkers of the world, and a question that you will almost certainly be asked time and time again. It is not within the scope of this book to take on the debate, even if I felt equal to the task, but some pertinent points are worth raising and considering. In many ways this question takes us back to the issue of belief that I discussed at the beginning of the chapter, an issue that creates an automatic division. In most people's minds, fate and free will are concepts that are both non-provable and mutually exclusive. If you believe in fate, it is assumed that you feel that your life is mapped out for you by a higher force, that it is out of your hands and beyond your control, for good or for bad. If you believe in free will, it is assumed that you believe in your own autonomy, that you are a free agent, and that the pattern of your life is dictated by your own ability to assess, choose, and decide.

As an astrologer and Tarot reader, I cannot deny the existence of fate. In the words of Liz Greene, the modern astrologer *"must sup with fate each time he considers a horoscope."* [6]

The fact that some kind of destiny is at work is borne out time and again by retrodiction—seeing how a horoscope has worked in the past—as well as by the possibility of prediction. However, to take the view that fate is an inexorable, unchangeable force is, in my view, both unhelpful and unhealthy simply because it promotes the idea that life happens "to" us. Taken to its logical conclusion, this line of thinking renders us all helpless puppets.

I personally feel that fate and free will are not mutually exclusive. However much our life events and relationships may be mapped out for us, there is, ultimately, a "so what?" factor because it is still up to us to deal with them. So much of human happiness and achievement comes down to motivation and empowerment that if free will is an illusion, it is at least a helpful one. Clients also often ask me if I believe in reincarnation. The answer is, yes, I do, but no matter what my arguments to support this belief may be, I am also aware of the fact that, no matter how many times I have already been here, and no matter how many more times I may come back, I only have this particular life this time around, and I would like to make the best possible job of it that I can.

CAUSALITY

Wrapped up in the notion of fate is the issue of causality—that some unseen force impels us to do certain things, behave in certain ways, be in particular places at particular times, and so on. A great deal of language, especially around astrology, is misleading in this sense. Countless times I have heard students and clients alike say, "Oh, my Venus is in Scorpio, that's why I get so passionate and jealous."

My answer to such statements is always the "chicken and egg" argument. In other words, which comes first? Are you passionate and jealous because your Venus is in Scorpio, or does your Venus in Scorpio reflect that you are passionate and jealous? The second angle has to be the correct one because the planets, themselves, do not make us do anything or behave in any particular way. They are not symbolic. Imbuing planets with symbolism is a human act of assignation of meaning and our horoscopes, therefore, are not autonomous pieces of machinery but mirrors. They reflect back to us, symbolically, how we find ourselves in the world. In short, we are our horoscopes and our horoscopes are us and there is no causal factor in play.

A popular metaphor is that fate is the hand we are dealt, while free will enables us to choose how we play it. This appeals to me because it allows us to take our place in the world without the limitations of being merely passive participants.

THE **TAROT** AND **ASTROLOGY**

You do not have to calculate the whole chart and be an expert astrologer in order to have astrology as an extra string to your bow. Significant astrological activity includes the transits of the planets and these are often reflected in a Tarot spread.

Learning the Glyphs
To use an Ephemeris you need to learn the glyphs (see pages 22–23 and 26). These are the astrologer's shorthand—symbols that represent the planets and signs.

It is not my intention to present a crash course in astrology, which is an enormous subject, but simply to show the nuts and bolts of the craft. In particular, learning how to pick out certain information will, hopefully, illustrate that you do not have to be an expert in astrology in order to use it alongside your Tarot readings. I have had clients for whom I have done both Tarot readings and horoscopes but, more usually, I have

no horoscope to refer to. Ephemerides—astrological tables—will tell you where the planets are for midday or midnight on any date and you can look up a client's date of birth on the spot.

TRANSITS

If you have the basic symbolism of the planets, the transits (where the planets are currently positioned) will tell their own story and are, more often than not,

Using the ephemerides

Using ephemerides will give you two lines of inquiry: firstly, you can look up a client's date of birth and see at a glance where the planets were at that time. Our Sun sign is our essence, but we are all, in fact, a mixture of signs. Check out the other planetary placings, especially from the Moon through to Saturn, to give you a bigger picture from the personality/ psychological point of view.

For example, you will see below that someone born on 1 April, 1968, has the Sun in Aries but the Moon in earthy Taurus, and both Mercury and Venus in sensitive Pisces.

APRIL 1968

Date	Sun	Moon	Mercury	Venus	Mars	Jupiter	Saturn	Uranus	Neptune	Pluto
1st	11 ♈ 20	14 ♉ 54	20 ♓ 01	20 ♓ 15	02 ♉ 57	26 ♌ 30	14 ♈ 51	26 ♍ 34	26 ♏ 14	21 ♍ 01
2nd	12 ♈ 19	26 ♉ 54	21 ♓ 37	21 ♓ 29	03 ♉ 41	26 ♌ 27	14 ♈ 58	26 ♍ 32	26 ♏ 13	20 ♍ 60
3rd	13 ♈ 18	08 ♊ 32	23 ♓ 14	22 ♓ 43	04 ♉ 25	26 ♌ 23	15 ♈ 06	26 ♍ 29	26 ♏ 12	20 ♍ 58
4th	14 ♈ 17	20 ♊ 24	24 ♓ 52	23 ♓ 57	05 ♉ 09	26 ♌ 20	15 ♈ 13	26 ♍ 27	26 ♏ 11	20 ♍ 57
5th	15 ♈ 16	02 ♋ 24	26 ♓ 32	25 ♓ 11	05 ♉ 53	26 ♌ 16	15 ♈ 21	26 ♍ 24	26 ♏ 10	20 ♍ 55
6th	16 ♈ 15	14 ♋ 37	28 ♓ 13	26 ♓ 25	06 ♉ 37	26 ♌ 13	15 ♈ 28	26 ♍ 22	26 ♏ 09	20 ♍ 54
7th	17 ♈ 14	27 ♋ 06	29 ♓ 56	27 ♓ 39	07 ♉ 21	26 ♌ 11	15 ♈ 36	26 ♍ 19	26 ♏ 07	20 ♍ 52
8th	18 ♈ 13	09 ♌ 56	01 ♈ 40	28 ♓ 53	08 ♉ 05	26 ♌ 08	15 ♈ 44	26 ♍ 17	26 ♏ 06	20 ♍ 51

reflected in the Tarot spread. For example, Uranus is synonymous with the Tower, as it spells upheaval, shock, things happening unexpectedly, or change being thrust upon us. It is also important to combine the symbolism of the two planets involved in a transit and you will find keywords for each planet at the end of this chapter.

EPHEMERIDES

Once you become familiar with using ephemerides, you will be able to date transits, from when they started to when they will finish. The most important factor to bear in mind is that planets can travel in retrograde motion—backtracking through a sign—as well as in direct motion, moving forward through a sign. Using the example below, Uranus travels backward and forward over 26 degrees of Aquarius from March 2002 to January 2003.

From the Ephemerides, you will see that there are ten columns, one for each planet, in the following order: Sun, Moon, Mercury, Venus, Mars, Jupiter, Saturn, Uranus, Neptune, and Pluto. Each line gives the sign, degree, and minute for each planet. For example, a midnight ephemeris will tell you that on 1 January, 2000, the Sun is at 09g 51—9 degrees and 51 minutes of Capricorn, the Moon at 07e17—7 degrees and 17 minutes of Scorpio, Mercury at 01g06—one degree and six minutes of Capricorn—and so on.

From the example below left, Uranus as the unexpected, contacting Jupiter, the planet of expansion, could signal an opportunity that comes out of the blue or an unplanned change of direction. We would expect to hear stories of being pushed into the fast lane, life becoming unpredictable, and the best-laid plans being suddenly subject to change.

Secondly, you can look up the current date and see where the planets are now. This will enable you to locate what are called *transits*, and the last five planets, Jupiter through to Pluto, are the most important in this respect.

For example, if the person born on 1 April, 1968, came to see me in March 2002, I would note that Uranus is at 26 degrees of Aquarius, and therefore transiting—or traveling—opposite this person's natal Jupiter, which was at 26 degrees of Leo at the time of birth.

MARCH 2002

Date	Sun	Moon	Mercury	Venus	Mars	Jupiter	Saturn	Uranus
7th	16 Pl 14	27 ♐ 27	22 ♒ 42	28 Pl 40	03 ♉ 48	05 ♋ 40	08 ♊ 42	26 ♒ 02
8th	17 Pl 14	10 ♑ 03	24 ♒ 07	29 Pl 55	04 ♉ 30	05 ♋ 41	08 ♊ 45	26 ♒ 05
9th	18 Pl 14	22 ♑ 24	25 ♒ 34	01 ♈ 09	05 ♉ 13	05 ♋ 43	08 ♊ 48	26 ♒ 08
10th	19 Pl 14	04 ♒ 34	27 ♒ 02	02 ♈ 24	05 ♉ 55	05 ♋ 44	08 ♊ 52	26 ♒ 12
11th	20 Pl 14	16 ♒ 35	28 ♒ 31	03 ♈ 39	06 ♉ 37	05 ♋ 46	08 ♊ 55	26 ♒ 15
12th	21 Pl 14	28 ♒ 32	00 Pl 02	04 ♈ 53	07 ♉ 19	05 ♋ 48	08 ♊ 58	26 ♒ 18
13th	22 Pl 14	10 Pl 26	01 Pl 33	06 ♈ 08	08 ♉ 01	05 ♋ 50	09 ♊ 02	26 ♒ 21
14th	23 Pl 14	22 Pl 18	03 Pl 06	07 ♈ 22	08 ♉ 44	05 ♋ 52	09 ♊ 05	26 ♒ 25

ASTROLOGICAL SIGNS

This chart is designed to give you a flavor of the signs and elements. The signs of the zodiac are in the following order, along with their main symbol and element. The glyphs are given for each sign and for their ruling planet(s).

ARIES
the ram

As the first sign of the zodiac, Aries represents the ego—"self"-ish and single-minded. As self-starters, the nature of Aries is to pioneer, initiate, and lead. Aries can be heard in the phrases "I am," and "me first," but as warriors they are defenders of the weak.
Ruling planet *Mars*

TAURUS
the bull

This earth sign is known for its solid connection with the material world, and the nature of Taurus is to acquire and consolidate. They seek safety, comfort, and familiarity. Taurus is sensuous, but there may be a tendency to stubbornness, laziness, or inertia.
Ruling planet *Venus*

GEMINI
the twins

Here is the communicator of the zodiac. Gemini loves to talk, debate, gossip, and tell jokes. The sign of the twins indicates duality, which can manifest as the ability to do more than one thing at a time. Gemini is quick, clever, a jack of all trades but master of none.
Ruling planet *Mercury*

CANCER
the crab

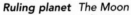

The home-maker, nurturer, and protector—clannish, family first. There is a fine line between being tenacious and clingy. Loving and caring on a good day; moody and changeable on a bad one. Like the crab there is a hard shell but a soft center.
Ruling planet *The Moon*

LEO
the lion

The show-off and entertainer of the zodiac. Bold, bossy, and loves a drama. Warm-hearted and generous. Loves to be at the heart of things and may tend to take over. Thrives when admired, but withers when unloved.
Ruling planet *The Sun*

VIRGO
the maiden

Exacting, precise, and analytical, Virgo pays attention to detail and tends to be economical with all resources. In the quest for perfection there is a tendency to criticize or expect too much, of oneself or of others. The sign of skills and crafts.
Ruling planet *Mercury*

This is the sign of partnership, relating, and arbitration. The sign of the scales symbolizes balance and cooperation, but also brings indecision. Sometimes called lazy Libra—can't be bothered. Seeks other people's opinions. A concern with harmony, beauty, and charm.
Ruling planet Venus

Intense, passionate, and determined, Scorpio is the opposite to superficial. A concern with in-depth issues, secrets, and power or control issues. The sign of regeneration, Scorpio knows how to start from scratch, but also knows how to heal.
Ruling planets Mars/Pluto

The traveler of the zodiac, either out in the world or within the mind. The explorer, philosopher, and seeker of truth. A concern with wisdom, justice, and freedom. Sometimes naive. A tendency to exaggerate or offend but with no malice intended.
Ruling planet Jupiter

Steady, realistic, and practical, Capricorns know how to pick their way to the summit. Like the mountain goat they are sure-footed and hardy. A concern with responsibility and authority, which is often experienced early in life. Sometimes pessimistic.
Ruling planet Saturn

The sign of the group as opposed to the individual. A concern with issues that affect people and the world at large. Great value attached to friendship. Intelligent, systematic, detached, objective —or quirky and eccentric.
Ruling planets Saturn/Uranus

The most sensitive of the signs. Pisces picks up on undercurrents and soaks up atmosphere—but getting it wrong can lead to paranoia. A powerful imagination creates the dreamers and artists of the world. Tends toward escapism, especially through addiction.
Ruling planets Jupiter/Neptune

LIBRA
the scales

SCORPIO
the scorpion

SAGITTARIUS
the centaur

CAPRICORN
the mountain goat

AQUARIUS
the water bearer

PISCES
the fishes

Key Characteristics of the Elements

FIRE

ARIES, LEO, SAGITTARIUS
energy, warmth, vision, intuition

EARTH

TAURUS, VIRGO, CAPRICORN
sensuality, fertility, practicality, materialism

AIR

GEMINI, LIBRA, AQUARIUS
thought, intellect, ideas, interaction

WATER

CANCER, SCORPIO, PISCES
sensitivity, feelings, empathy, instinct

THE **PLANETS**

Each planet travels through the 12 signs of the zodiac at different speeds. According to the planet's cycle, it returns to the same position within a specific period of time. In this way, we all experience Jupiter returns every 12 years, but none of us will ever experience a Neptune or Pluto return.

For planets with longer cycles, such as Neptune or Pluto, the quarter, and especially the half, points of these periods of time are important. The information below sets out the returns of the different planets and when we will experience them.

SYMBOLISM OF THE PLANETS

Sun Ego, essence, spirit, consciousness. Vitality, general health, and constitution. The masculine principle—men, fathers, male authority. Objectivity. Gold, light, and heat. Rules the back, especially the spine, and the heart.

Moon Emotions, needs, gut reactions, and habitual responses. The feminine principle—women, mothers, the maternal instinct. Receptivity, the unconscious. Menstruation, babies, small children. Rules the stomach and the womb.

Mercury Everything to do with communication—expression, speech, language, letters, books, the media, lies, truth. Jokes, tricks, and cunning. Early learning. Local neighborhood. Local travel and means of transport. Rules the lungs, hands, nervous and respiratory system.

Venus Women and all that is feminine. Love, lovers, sex, pleasure—seeking of all kinds. Romance, the arts, beauty, attraction, and attractiveness. Relating, social skills. Nature, money, food— especially sweet things. Adornment. Rules the kidneys and throat.

Mars Men and all that is masculine. War, soldiers, combat, and all things military. Drive, energy, action, motivation, push and shove. Initiative, will, desire, lust, courage. Anger, accidents, violence, danger, alarms.

Planet cycles
The slower-moving planets (Jupiter, Saturn, Uranus, Neptune, and Pluto) are most important in terms of transits:

THE SUN
The Sun takes a year to return to the same position, so your birthday is your Solar Return—hence "Many happy returns of the day."

THE MOON
28 days

MERCURY

VENUS
Approximately one year

MARS
Two years

Surgery, knives, and needles. Pain, cuts, wounds, scars, fevers, infections, inflammation. Rules the face and skull.

Jupiter All the "ex's"—expansion, exaggeration, extravagance, excess, exuberance. Generosity, charity, protection, preservation. Freedom, liberation, emancipation. Enthusiasm, optimism, celebration. Luck, opportunity, and risk-taking. Long-distance travel and all things foreign. The law, justice, fairness. Higher education, wisdom, knowledge. Religion, faith, ethics. Rules the hips, thighs, liver, blood, sciatic nerve.

Saturn Boundaries, barriers, structures, restriction, and limitation. Delays and denial. Responsibility, discipline, duty, and work. All that is conventional and safe. Caution and control. Pessimism, gravity, sobriety, and reality. Age, time, and death. Rules the skin, the teeth, the bones, and especially the knees.

Uranus All that is unexpected or erratic—suddenness, shocks, rebellion, revolution, disruption. The bizarre, the unconventional. Controversy, dissociation, splitting. Explosions, accidents, earthquakes. Electricity, computers, technology, machinery. Groups, society, ecology. Idealism, communism, anarchy. Associated with the ankles.

Neptune The world of fantasy and the imagination—daydreams, illusion. Confusion, uncertainty, and lies. Idealization, glamor. The arts, especially film, the stage, poetry, music. Dreams and sleep. Addictive substances. Sacrifice, suffering, loss. Symbiosis, the urge to merge. Mysticism, spiritualism. Fogs, mists. Everything to do with the sea and marine life. Associated with the feet.

Pluto Absence, loss, destruction, annihilation. Total change through the painful process of symbolic death, rebirth, and transformation. Power and control. All that is hidden, black, or invisible. The unconscious, psychoanalysis. Obsessions, intensity, depression. Elimination. Deep healing. Associated with the sexual organs.

JUPITER
12 years

SATURN
29.5 years

URANUS
76–84 years

NEPTUNE
178 years

PLUTO
248 years

SUN
Dignity: *Leo*
Detriment: *Aquarius*
Exaltation: *Aries* Fall: *Libra*

MOON
Dignity: *Cancer*
Detriment: *Capricorn*
Exaltation: *Taurus* Fall: *Scorpio*

MERCURY
Dignity: *Gemini, Virgo*
Detriment: *Sagittarius, Pisces*
Exaltation: *Virgo* Fall: *Pisces*

VENUS
Dignity: *Taurus, Libra*
Detriment: *Scorpio, Aries*
Exaltation: *Pisces* Fall: *Virgo*

MARS
Dignity: *Aries, Scorpio*
Detriment: *Libra, Taurus*
Exaltation: *Capricorn* Fall: *Cancer*

JUPITER
Dignity: *Sagittarius, Pisces*
Detriment: *Gemini, Virgo*
Exaltation: *Cancer* Fall: *Capricorn*

SATURN
Dignity: *Capricorn, Aquarius*
Detriment: *Cancer, Leo*
Exaltation: *Libra* Fall: *Aries*

URANUS
Dignity: *Co-ruler of Aquarius*
Detriment: *Leo*
Exaltation: *—* Fall: *—*

NEPTUNE
Dignity: *Co-ruler of Pisces*
Detriment: *Virgo*
Exaltation: *—* Fall: *—*

PLUTO
Dignity: *Co-ruler of Scorpio*
Detriment: *Taurus*
Exaltation: *—* Fall: *—*

PLANETS

The following information tells you where planets are at their most or their least effective:

Dignity When a planet is in dignity, it means that it is in the sign, or one of the signs, that it rules. The planet is "at home" and working in harmony with the sign.

Detriment When a planet is in detriment, it means that it is in the opposite sign or signs to the ones it rules. The planet is in conflict with the sign.

Exaltation When a planet is in its sign of exaltation, it means that it is at its most powerful. It shows the perfect union, with the planet bringing out the best qualities of that sign.

Fall When a planet is in fall, it means that it is in the sign opposite to its sign of exaltation. It shows a mismatch and a conflict of interests.

Locating significance
Whether the planets are in dignity, detriment, exaltation, or fall helps the astrologer to assess the degree of harmony or conflict within each particular horoscope.

INFORMATION VERSUS MEANING

If you are a complete beginner, there is very little substitute for information-gathering as your first step. Learning the traditional meanings of the cards is an obvious starting point.

After you have learned the traditional meanings of the cards, you may then decide to study all the 78 cards one by one, or in pairs or groups. Many books then advise meditation and reflection on each card in order to connect with the images and ideas it suggests to you. This is an excellent way to start if this method appeals to you, and you are able to meditate on the card without your mind wandering off on tangents.

It is difficult to remember exactly how my learning process evolved. I read as much as I could, but the best exercise was constantly looking at the cards and doing readings for anyone who would let me.

CREATIVE LEARNING

Where do you go from there? Compiling lists of keywords or possible meanings is tempting, and this approach can certainly play a useful role in the early stages. However, making notes can only take you so far and can quickly become heavy-going and flat, so don't get carried away. This takes you back to the problem inherent in attempts to assign predetermined meanings. Remember the dream analogy and start by looking for the manifest content—the themes of the card—and allow yourself to trust that the latent content will emerge once a card appears within the context of a reading.

Many students tend to give up when they approach the difficulty of interpreting spreads, that is, the different combinations of cards. The same stumbling block exists in astrology. Learning the mechanics of chart calculation and grasping the basic meaning of the signs, planets, houses, and aspects is relatively easy, but interpretation of each individual horoscope is another matter, as every chart is unique. Every Tarot spread is also unique. This is easily illustrated by the fact that, if you take just the Celtic Cross, the traditional ten-card layout, a statistician will tell you that, working with 78 cards, you are up against 1,258,315,963,905 possible spreads. You are more likely to win the lottery—a one in 14 million chance—than you are of getting the same spread twice.

So, we cannot possibly learn every combination in advance. This is the point. Even if we could memorize thousands of combinations, it wouldn't mean that we would be expert Tarot readers. On the contrary, we would have fallen into the trap of amassing information with no meaning. No Tarot spread or horoscope means anything until it is addressed along with the querent—the person seeking the consultation. Every reading needs a context, and that context is the uniqueness of the life, the question, the situation, the relationship, and so on, of the querent.

Don't categorize
However you enter into the Tarot world, remember that your goal is to familiarize yourself with the cards. There are no right or wrong answers and the most important thing is to not turn the information-gathering exercise into a laborious process. If a certain card doesn't speak to you, then move on to the next one. Keep your imagination alive and don't try to categorize.

The word Arcana is derived from the word "arcane," which means hidden, secret, or mysterious. The Major Arcana, as the name suggests, comprises the most important cards of the Tarot pack. These cards make up the first 22 cards of the pack and are numbered 0 to 21, from the Fool through to the World.

THE MAJOR ARCANA

2

the **Fool**

The Fool does not mean "idiot" and neither is he foolish in the sense that we now use the word, that is, for someone who lacks judgment or vision. As the first card of the Major Arcana the Fool symbolizes a beginning or a fresh start.

THE FOOL

Traditional meaning
A beginning, a journey.

When the Fool comes up in a spread it can indicate that a return to simplicity, a child-like state, is called for. It may be necessary to detach from worldly values, or to let go of the past, in order to embrace big life changes.

Inevitably, this picture includes an element of risk in the face of change, but only once the need for change is accepted can you look at your options and choose. Do you dare start again?

There is also an issue of planning—or not planning—with the Fool. A child lives almost entirely in the present moment, maybe looking ahead five minutes but certainly not five years or even months. So the Fool can indicate spontaneity, an unplanned turn of events that sets you on a new path. To a large extent, there is the need to jump in at the deep end and to be open to new experiences and new possibilities. It may be a case of deciding not to keep waiting for the right time as this may never arise. Humans are expert at finding reasons for delaying so that they can stay in their safety zone, even if that is the worst place for them.

Leaving that safety zone is what it's all about. For some people it will feel like jumping out of an aircraft without a parachute. For others the prospect of a new cycle can be exhilarating. Either way, the Fool tells you that it is time to be on the move and to find the right path. The Fool is not a stationary figure. He is a seeker, a traveler—but he does not stay in five-star hotels. He owns nothing but the clothes he stands up in and the few belongings tied up in his knapsack.

This doesn't mean that you should give away all your worldly goods. But it does mean that you should maybe attach less

The Fool can represent a journey, both literally and symbolically, showing a need for change.

importance to them. The message in setting aside your material world is that it enables you to discover who you really are and what you really want. Self-realization is the goal, and it is a journey you must undertake alone.

NAIVE WISDOM

The other image that is conjured up by the Fool is the one who plays the fool, like the court jester. But it is the subtle side to the jester that is important, rather than his buffoonery:

> *"As the court jester he was seen as possessing a naive wisdom that made him wiser at times than those around him.... The fool, like Socrates, was wise enough to know that he knew nothing.... In the Tarot, the Fool is that part of ourselves that is wise enough to stand*

Interpreting the Fool

The Fool is universal man and woman, starting the journey through life. His number is zero, so he is like a blank canvas or a clean page. He is inexperienced and child-like in that he represents a state of naivety untainted by cynicism. The mood is one of hope and optimism, as conjured up by the details of the card—the carefree figure with his knapsack slung over his shoulder, face uplifted toward the shining sun, the dog at his heels, new vistas opening up around him.

> *awestruck before the mystery of creation, and bold enough to set off exploring."* [7]

Just as children can astound us with their insights, so can the Fool speak to that part of us that still knows the difference between truth and artifice, that rises above our conditioning and sees things for what they really are.

Links to Astrology
We can liken the Fool to the Spring Equinox, 0° of Aries, the beginning of a whole new cycle. Aries is the first sign of the zodiac, symbolizing the ego and expressed in the language of "I am." In character the Fool may also be described by the fire sign Sagittarius. He is the traveler of the zodiac, expressed in the language of "I seek." Sagittarius hunts out new experiences and wisdom and approaches life with child-like optimism.

The Fool invariably comes up when you need to make a clean break from a way of life, such as a dead-end job or relationship. This was the case with a young woman who was living abroad and trying to build a life with a foreign man. She was besotted with him but, unfortunately, he could not commit as he would never marry outside of his own race and culture.

In her reading the Fool came up as the outcome card, pointing in this case to both a literal journey and the break with her current lifestyle. Within weeks of the reading she had packed her backpack and returned to England to start her life anew. This was not easy for her but, a few months later, she took up a new profession in which she proved to be highly successful.

I the **Magician**

THE MAGICIAN

When this card comes up in a reading it often indicates that there are possibilities or opportunities around you that are about to surface or that you haven't noticed.

You may need to recognize your own skills and to focus on developing them, or you may need to recognize your own power. With this card I encourage the client to ask, "What am I good at? In what way am I underestimating myself?"

It may also be that someone has lost sight of the magic of life. I always try to communicate the uplifting quality of this card—life can be magical, you can create your own magic and bring your own willpower into play. There is a whole reservoir of positive energy here just waiting to be tapped, and it is closer or easier to do than you might think. When the Magician appears it promises developments and the chance to transform a relationship or a situation. Change may come from within you, such as a shift in attitude, desire, or belief, or it may come

Traditional meaning
Skill, confidence,
communication.

The Magician came up as the immediate future card in a reading for a young woman who was deliberating about starting her own business. Through this card we were able to explore the different skills and resources that she would need to harness in order to begin.

She already had the Wands—the vision, the enthusiasm, and the willingness to learn and explore. In the Swords we located both the idea for her business and the drive to make it happen, and she admitted to an element of self-doubt, which was partly responsible for delays. The Cups spoke of her desire to do something she loved and to be her own boss. The Pentacles symbolized the capital she would need, and at the time of the reading, she had no idea where this was going to come from.

It was clear that she needed to research the financial market, approach her bank or maybe seek out an organization that helped new businesses get on their feet. Other Pentacles cards in the spread suggested she would find the funding she needed and I urged her to press on without further delay. I felt that once she found somebody else to believe in her and her project, she would start believing in herself and her business, too, and that it would happen.

in the shape of news or another outside factor which will rearrange the picture. There is a correlation between the Magician and the planet Mercury, who in Greek mythology is Hermes, the winged messenger of the gods. So this card can indicate that new information is about to surface and may already be winging its way toward you.

The Magician can also represent another person in your life and, as with the Pages, Knights, and Kings in the Court cards, there is no rule that this person has to be male. It is more important to let the cards describe a *type* of person, and whoever is signified by the Magician will be somebody clever, powerful, quick, skilled, and persuasive. Notice that above the Magician's head there hovers a lemniscate, the sideways figure of eight that is the symbol of infinity. This reinforces the message that the Magician is set apart from the ordinary mortal world. He represents a god-like figure who knows the deepest secrets and mysteries of life.

In this respect the Magician is a healer, so he may appear in the guise of a doctor or some kind of therapist. He is a good omen if you are dealing with health questions, as he indicates that help is on the way, or that the right help is out there and can be sought. Alternative health remedies may need to be considered as an holistic approach is called for—the need to combine the physical with the metaphysical, to recognize that your physical wellbeing is wrapped up with your spiritual health.

Interpreting the Magician

How exciting that the first person we encounter on our journey is the Magician, a card rich with possibilities. If you look on his table you can see that he has one of each four suits—a Wand, a Pentacle, a Sword, and a Cup. The four suits of the Tarot correspond to the four elements of fire, earth, air, and water, which in turn symbolize the four essential qualities of life—our energy and initiative, the material world and the senses, our intellect and ideas, and our emotional needs and responses. All are represented here, so part of the Magician's purpose is to tell us that all the resources we need are available to us—it is just a question of finding them, recognizing them, and learning how to use them to our best advantage.

Links to Astrology

The Magician is well described by Mercury, the planet that rules everything connected with the written or spoken word, and it rules Gemini, the communicator of the zodiac. This sign is versatile, dexterous, quick-witted, clever, and inventive—all qualities possessed by the Magician.

Mercury also rules Virgo, an earth sign known for being hard-working, analytical, precise, and thorough. Virgo belongs to the sixth house, the sector of the horoscope that rules work, craft, skills, and health. Again, the combination of Mercury in Virgo is a fitting astrological analogy for the Magician.

the **High Priestess**

THE HIGH PRIESTESS

This card is sometimes called the Papess and she is partnered with The Hierophant, sometimes called the Pope, the only cards in the Tarot with religious connotations.

In a patriarchal world it is the male figurehead who holds power and authority in organized religion, such as the Pope in the Catholic faith. And as male supremacy escalated throughout history, so female spiritual power became something to fear and eventually something to be stamped out, hence the notorious witch hunts of the past. In the Tarot, however, no such inequality exists and the High Priestess holds her own undisputed place in a world that recognizes the need for all types of beliefs, attitudes, and differences to be represented.

As a benign figure, the High Priestess is a person with highly developed intuition, someone who can counsel and give advice, someone to be listened to. She may be a modern day astrologer, tarot card reader, palmist, or therapist. Her spiritual wisdom enables her to divine, heal, or guide. She can represent someone who steers and supports us and someone who puts us back in touch with who we really are. She also

Traditional meaning Secrets, that which is hidden, the power of spiritual wisdom.

The Three of Swords (heartache) was the center card crossed by the Knight of Cups (suitor), in a spread for a woman in her mid-thirties. Clearly there was a man involved around whom there was considerable pain or sadness. The High Priestess signified the near future and so I felt that this must be a man who was already involved with someone else and that here was one of those tortuous triangles, which she confirmed.

She told me that he had given her many reasons for not wanting to get married but that they had been fabrications, as the real obstacle to commitment was a long–term girlfriend, whom he had neglected to mention from the outset. By this time, my client was hooked and wanted to know if there was any future in the relationship.

I described the High Priestess and how I felt that she was indicating the girlfriend, the presence of a woman in a position of great power, who knew things that my client didn't and who should by no means be underestimated. Other cards in the spread pointed to frustrated desires, so the answer to her question had to be no.

knows things that we are not aware of and secrets yet to be revealed.

As a malign figure she is still a powerful person, but unfathomable. There is more to this person than meets the eye or than we've been led to believe. Sometimes she is the "other" man or woman—the third party in a triangular setup. But whatever her exact role may be, her power is not to be underestimated, as she can be a fearsome adversary and, again, is aware of things that we are not. At worst this is someone who abuses his or her position of power, someone who is scheming or driven by the need to control. Be on the lookout for stories of obsessive behavior or emotional blackmail.

Alternatively, the High Priestess can symbolize the highly receptive, feminine power within us, the witch in all of us, whose magical gifts and qualities can show us another way of looking at the world. She asks us to be still, to go deeper, and to look and feel beyond the obvious. She symbolizes the mysteries of life and reigns over that which cannot be seen, the invisible rather than the visible, so we may need to look deep inside ourselves for answers and insights rather than to the outside world.

In a situation this card can mean that information will slowly come to light that will give you a different perspective. There is a need to trust in the process of time and, for some, there may be an element of spiritual enlightenment and personal growth as a particular situation unfolds.

Interpreting the High Priestess

The High Priestess sits at the entrance to the temple, between two pillars that are inscribed with the initials B and J, which stand for Boaz and Jachin. Why these names were given and what they signify is a matter of dispute and it is not within the scope of this book to explore the history of the cards. In terms of learning the message of the card, the most important point is that one pillar is black and the other white, representing masculine/feminine or yang/yin. As the High Priestess holds the space between the pillars, and is assigned the number two card in the Major Arcana sequence, we can see her as a uniting principle, a force which can tolerate ambiguity and contain polarities.

Her "witchiness" is symbolized by a large crescent of the New Moon at her feet. But, as a witch, her power can be used either constructively or destructively, and whether the High Priestess is a benign or malign influence is decided by her position in the spread and the nature of the surrounding cards.

Links to Astrology
The High Priestess is the ultimate in the feminine principle. Associated with the Moon, she taps into fluid, female energy.

In character she correlates to a Scorpio, as she has the positive face of this sign—psychic insights, healing ability, and strength. But she can also have the negative side—jealousy and the tendency to abuse power.

III the **Empress**

The Empress is the ultimate Earth Mother, soft, womanly, beautiful, and fertile, close to nature and abundance, and representing matter and the physical rather than spirit.

THE EMPRESS

Traditional meaning
Fertility,
motherhood.

In my experience, questions about motherhood and babies are common and this is a powerful card in terms of signaling pregnancy or a recent or imminent birth, either for the client or for someone close to her (or him). However, I tend to avoid readings for the question, "Will I ever have a child?" as, more often than not, it is a question of wistfulness and there are other factors to be sorted out before parenthood can be considered. Also, the client may not be ready to hear a resounding no. For many women a negative answer to this question would be upsetting, even devastating, so it is

important to tread carefully. But if a client is already pregnant, or trying to conceive, then the Empress is a very positive card for predicting conception or the arrival of a healthy child. She is also an extremely helpful card for warning someone about pregnancy if they are not planning it.

But the Empress is more than mother, she is lover too. Her sensuality and sexuality are part of her richness. The glyph for Venus is on the heart-shaped shield at her feet, a glyph used universally as a symbol for women, just as the Mars glyph is used for men. The Empress is linked to Venus, Aphrodite, goddess of love and beauty. She is the loved woman— valued and cherished. She does not belong to casual relationships or to those based on lust rather than love. She is a whole woman—warm, sexy, nurturing, and stable. This is an excellent card to see when dealing with questions of love and marriage, as she tells us that it is the real thing—healthy love and sexuality rather than infatuation, obsession, or a mistake.

If this card appears in a spread asking about a situation, then it points to the matter being fruitful and productive. Rewards and satisfaction are promised.

The Empress can signal a pregnancy or an imminent birth. It can also embody the mother figure and the best of women.

The Empress has appeared many times in the context of questions about love, marriage, and children and is generally a wonderful omen for contentment. However, in one reading for a young woman with a baby, the Empress crossed the King of Swords in the middle of the Celtic Cross. I asked her if she was feeling unloved since the birth of her child, which she immediately confirmed with floods of tears.

It is not an uncommon story. Two people fall madly in love, have a wonderful wedding and are full of joy at the prospect of the first baby. The reality of parenthood then brings them back down to earth and, in this case, the strain on the marriage was enormous. She now experienced her husband as cold and unfeeling—the King of Swords—while she was struggling to cope with her first child as well as trying to recapture her place in his life as the loved woman. She now felt that being his wife and the mother of his child had fallen horribly short of her dreams.

Happily, other cards in the spread pointed to togetherness and success and I was able to assure her that love was still there on both sides and that this was a classic "bad patch." In her heart she already knew that they would work through their problems, but this was a good example of how a reading can be an effective therapy session. The reading brought her a great deal of comfort and she went away reassured and with renewed hope for the future.

Interpreting the Empress

Just as the High Priestess symbolizes the mystical and magical powers of the feminine principle—the metaphysical—the Empress symbolizes the physical. She sits on her throne amidst lush vegetation, richly dressed in a robe covered with pomegranates, a fruit sacred to Demeter [8] the earth mother and which symbolize fertility. Interestingly, pomegranates are also to be found with the High Priestess, indicating the fecundity of both spiritual and physical development.

Links to Astrology

The Empress is clearly aligned with Venus, the planet of love and pleasure, and she rules the sensual earth sign of Taurus. People with Venus in Taurus love food, money, sex, and shopping and will use any or all of these to excess if love is absent.

Between them the High Priestess and the Empress correlate to the Scorpio–Taurus polarity. Scorpio is linked to all that is dark, mysterious, hidden, invisible, or risky. Taurus symbolizes the exact opposite—all that can be seen, touched, felt, and tasted, and all that is safe, satisfying, and obvious.

IV the **Emperor**

THE EMPEROR

Traditional meaning
*Authority, power,
leadership,
ambition, reason.*

A stern-looking man sits on a throne decorated with rams' heads. There is something of the warrior about him as his red robes cloak his suit of armor, but his golden and bejeweled crown and the scepter in his right hand also show him to be regal. The long grey beard suggests the wisdom of age and experience.

Here is the partner card to the Empress and, just as the Empress can embody mother and the best of women, so can the Emperor embody father, the best of men, and the masculine principle. At best here is someone who is judicious, unbiased, level-headed, someone who holds strong principles and values, especially toward his family or other loved ones, and is someone we look up to.

When this card appears in a reading it often means that the triumph of head over heart is called for. Logic is needed rather than an emotional or intuitive response, because what you want is not necessarily what you need. Objectivity rather than subjectivity will give you a clearer and more accurate picture. This card can also signal some tough decision-making and the need to stick to your guns and to stand up for yourself. There may be issues around claiming your own authority in a situation or within a relationship.

These issues are especially likely to apply to women, as the Emperor can represent a strong patriarchal figure, for example in father/daughter relationships. At worst, this card can describe someone

The Emperor can embody a father figure and the best of men. He holds strong family values and is someone you can look up to.

who is intelligent but too conventional, strong-minded but inflexible, and inclined to preach or control. He is difficult to appeal to, especially within a relationship, as he cannot reveal his vulnerability. He is not necessarily unkind in a deliberate way, but he is so tough, determined, disciplined, and self-reliant that he expects others to be the same way. As a result he ends up with his emotions hermetically sealed and he is never wrong. He has made the rules and expects everyone to stick to them, even if he doesn't.

Apart from representing this stereotype in human relationships, the Emperor can also be someone in a position of authority, such as a boss, a parent, or a business associate. The level of power that this person holds, and to what extent it is helpful or destructive, needs to be determined by the other cards that show in the spread.

Links to Astrology

Aries is the sign of the Ram so the rams' heads on the Emperor's throne connect him with this sign. Aries symbolizes the ego and a powerful drive to assert the self. Aries people are generally self-starters, leaders, and initiators, and hate to be contradicted or to come second. Ruled by Mars, the planet of war and action, here is the sign of the competitor, the warrior, the campaigner. There is also a case for linking the Emperor with Saturn, the planet of age and gravitas.

The Emperor would appear every time in several readings I did for a woman throughout her late twenties. A card will often reappear in different spreads in one session, demanding to be seen, but when it appears repeatedly in separate readings it shows a major focus.

In this case the Emperor was unmistakably the woman's father, who "loved" her but who controlled her by being over-protective and dictating her future. He wanted her to stay involved in the family business whereas she was constantly hankering to strike out for herself. She was exceptionally sensitive and intelligent, and capable of far more than the family business demanded of her. Not surprisingly, she suffered from severe depression which, despite years of therapy, continued to cast a shadow over her life. Her father's response was always "pull yourself together."

We explored the symbolism and the message of the Emperor several times and she didn't need to be convinced that his constant reappearance was telling her that he represented her biggest obstacle and challenge. I was convinced that her depression was a response to and a defense against her upbringing. We both knew that she would never find her autonomy and the path to improved mental health until she could stand up to her father. To do this without losing the relationship, she had to be able to appeal to his reason and not expect him to empathize with her. Ultimately, she needed to address the fact that he might never relinquish his role in the way that she would like him to. If there are people or situations that we cannot change, then all we can do is change our response, and this can be incredibly empowering.

This example shows the Emperor card working at two levels: on the surface as an obvious significator for her father, but at another level indicating the psychological issues involved. It showed how she would need to become more assertive in order to make a physical and psychological separation from her father.

the **Hierophant**

THE HIEROPHANT

Traditional meaning
*Spiritual advisor,
teacher.*

The Hierophant is sometimes called the Pope and the religious connotations of the card are obvious. A richly robed figure, wearing an ornate golden crown, gives audience to two clerics. He raises his right hand in a blessing while in his left he holds the triple-tiered Papal Cross.

I always used to find the Hierophant one of the most difficult cards to interpret and it is a good example of how we must not allow ourselves to be constrained by traditional meanings. The Hierophant is traditionally a spiritual advisor or teacher. Occasionally, you may do a reading for someone who does have a spiritual or religious mentor, but generally this idea will be met with blankness or laughter.

However, spirituality does not necessarily mean God or organized religion. Spirituality can simply mean an awareness of that other dimension to life, a realization that we are all bound to one another in some sense, which gives us a moral and ethical sense of responsibility toward our fellow human beings.

In many ways our spirituality is deeply connected to how we find meaning in life and how we separate right from wrong. This is what separates us from other sentient beings. In this sense the Hierophant can be a symbolic dig in the ribs, reminding us to get in touch with our own spiritual values and to be honest. The message is to live our own truth and not to fall into the trap of being spiritually or morally lazy.

As another person in your life the Hierophant has come to represent someone who is spiritually aware, experienced, and wise, and who is able to pass on the benefit of his or her experience and wisdom in all kinds of ways. This card stands for someone you look up to, someone you can trust with personal issues and someone whose advice you would actively seek and follow.

When this card appears in a reading, it may represent a teacher, a counselor, a therapist, or any kind of consultant. Or it

The Hierophant often represents a spiritual advisor or teacher, or someone who is spiritually aware and wise.

may represent your best friend or a loved one in whom you have faith and who has your best interests at heart.

Sometimes it may be the client who is the Hierophant, who is being asked to take up the role of advisor or to guide a situation down the right road. If the card is surrounded by other difficult cards, the message is to be wary of handing out advice, especially if it is unsolicited, and not to be high-handed or judgmental. You must not preach or allow yourself to be preached to. The Hierophant is also a helpful card for the Tarot reader, reminding us not to climb onto our soapbox or dish out esoteric jargon which is useful to nobody.

Links to Astrology

To me the Hierophant is Mercury, the winged messenger of the gods and the planet of language and communication. When he is well-placed he is like Mercury in his own signs of Gemini—dexterous and expert at discourse and providing information—or Virgo—analytical, careful, and intelligent. When he is ill-placed he may be like Mercury in his signs of detriment, Sagittarius and Pisces, in which there is a greater risk of a tendency to preach, to offer up platitudes, or to speak without thinking first.

The Hierophant is not necessarily an old sage. He or she can be any age and it is the type of character, or the role that he or she fulfills, which is of most importance.

In a reading for a man in his fifties the Hierophant turned out to be easily recognizable as his boss, a man ten years his junior. In spite of the age gap the client admired his boss and had the utmost respect for his judgment and vision. He was both happy and thankful to be guided by him, a guidance which extended into his personal life too, as his boss had also become a friend who was "amazingly supportive in every way."

In another reading I laid a spread for a woman in her early forties who was going through a divorce. She had been the one to leave and, although her husband had been devastated at the time, he had rallied relatively quickly and been just as keen as she to keep things amicable and civilized. Then, all of a sudden, things turned nasty and he wanted an immediate divorce and financial settlement. He had hastily put together a package with his solicitor and she was under a great deal of pressure to sign the agreement, which was heavily in his favor. Her question was should she sign and accept the sum being offered, even though it was far less than she was entitled to, and just get on with her life? Or should she take heed of her misgivings and suspicions and enter into legal proceedings, which surely promised to be messy, bitter, and prolonged?

The immediate future card was the Hierophant, so I suggested that she needed guidance and that nothing should be finalized without expert advice. At a later date she informed me that a close friend had put her in touch with a solicitor who was an expert in matrimonial law and that she was on the point of a settlement that was more than double the original offer.

VI the Lovers

I have invariably found that the Lovers card is pointing to a relationship or a meaningful love affair. It is a sexual card and it can indicate a powerful physical attraction, reminding us of the strong link between desire, passion, and love.

THE LOVERS

If a client has never had a Tarot reading before and is completely unfamiliar with the cards you can be sure that he or she will know this one, if only because he or she saw Roger Moore seduce Jane Seymour in the James Bond film with a Tarot pack in which all 78 cards were the Lovers.

This card can suggest a choice between platonic love and carnal knowledge. This meaning most often arises if someone is starting to fall for a person who is already a friend. It is the theme of, "I don't want to

risk spoiling what we already have," and the pros and cons need to be looked at carefully in such scenarios.

One possible problem with this card is if it arises within the context of an affair, when someone has set their heart on a person who is already spoken for or when someone who is already in a relationship is tempted by an extra-marital affair. Should he or she resist plucking the apple of temptation? The element of choice becomes a lot stronger—holding back or

Traditional meaning
Love and partnership, choice.

The Lovers appeared in a reading for a woman in her early twenties who was desperate to know if the man she was attracted to felt the same way about her. Sometimes she thought he was just being friendly and at other times she felt that he wanted more than friendship. Then she would wonder if she were just imagining it and the circle of questioning and wondering would start all over again. He was still with another partner but everyone had told her that this relationship was on its last legs.

I laid the seven-card relationship spread and it was one of the best I have ever seen. The significator for him was the Lovers card, so I told her that friendship was blossoming into something much more powerful and that she wasn't imagining the chemistry between them. The outcome card was the Ten of Cups— ultimate joy and happiness—and it is a wonderful moment for a Tarot reader to tell someone that they are about to get their heart's desire. In this case the results were rapid, as I had a call the following week to tell me that they were together, and a year later they were married.

becoming lovers, denying desire or giving in to it, battling with frustration or guilt, and so on.

In my experience, the situations which should be avoided are nearly always shown by much heavier cards such as the Devil. The Lovers card normally points to the right decision being made and to the birth of a wonderful new partnership, often with a true soul mate.

Interpreting the Lovers

Unless there are a lot of difficult cards to negate the Lovers, this card is usually an excellent omen for a relationship, especially one that is about to start or that is in the honeymoon phase in which the loved one can do no wrong and everything is perfect. What lies ahead is another matter, but for the time being everything in the garden is rosy. An angel, or Cupid in other packs, presides and a union or partnership is blessed.

If you compare the Lovers with the Devil card, you see the same image of a man and woman, side by side, in the presence of a powerful force. The Devil is the flip side of the Lovers, the shadow side of love, but the Lovers is a beautiful picture of love and light, where mutual attraction is strong.

Links to Astrology

In planetary terms the Lovers is Venus— Aphrodite—goddess of love, relating, and beauty. Venus rules Taurus, as seen with the Empress, and also Libra, the sign of the scales, which represents partnership and connections to a significant other. Venus in Libra symbolizes romance and relating, for which the keywords are togetherness, cooperation, and companionship.

The Lovers often represents a new relationship, where there is strong mutual attraction.

the **Chariot**

THE CHARIOT

The Charioteer is a skilled, competent character, standing in command of, not horses, but two sphinxes, one black and one white. His skill lies in mastering different forces simultaneously in order to make progress.

When the Chariot appears in a reading it often signifies different factors in a situation, factors that may be causing conflict and need to be juggled and controlled. One of the main messages of this card is about regaining control. The Chariot is our modern-day car and it is time to get back in the driving seat. Clever navigation and steering the right course can overcome obstacles and lead to success. It may simply be a matter of needing to find a new sense of direction, either in life or in a particular situation, or to find ways in which to harness your ambition. Or it may be that you need to recognize your power and authority in terms of how to take more control and become a driving force. Do you need to grab the reins and take an active role rather than a passive one?

Traditional meaning
Triumph, victory,
travel.

The Chariot can literally signify a vehicle. It has appeared several times in a spread when someone was due to take a driving test or had bought a new car. The best example was the Chariot appearing as the outcome card for a woman who was emigrating with her husband and two small children. What was their planned mode of transport? They had decided to drive from England to Greece in an old school bus that her husband had renovated into a mobile home.

In a relationship spread for a woman in her early thirties the Chariot appeared as the sixth card, the short-term future. The preceding card was the Ten of Wands (burdens) and the outcome card was the Seven of Wands (self–protection)—the picture was not very encouraging. I told her that I thought she had a fight on her hands. It turned out to be another complicated triangle situation, as she was seeing a man who was still tied up with his ex-girlfriend.

The Chariot was a welcome sight. If she couldn't change the situation, how could she change the way she was handling it? She realized that there weren't any boundaries in her relationship. This man called round to see her and phoned her at any time. She had fallen into the trap of keeping her time free for him, her friends were falling like flies and she had lost sight of calling some of the shots. She accepted that she needed to pick up the reins and get her life back on track.

The Chariot often indicates that there is movement or development in any situation that has been stuck or that has appeared to be out of your hands. The opportunity to move things on is there and often it is a question of finding the courage or the confidence to be more assertive. This is an important point to remember as, even though the Charioteer is a forceful and competitive character, he is not aggressive. Like the sphinxes he controls he is subtle, asserting the strength of his personality and charisma without resorting to heavy-handed tactics. Action is clever and calculated rather than reckless or ruthless. When the Chariot appears he is urging strategy first and action second.

At a more literal level the Chariot can signify travel, but it is usually a journey with a purpose rather than just a holiday. The Charioteer is highly focused and moves for a reason, with his goals always clearly in sight.

Interpreting the Chariot

The sphinxes with the Charioteer are commonly referred to as the opposing forces of good and evil within human nature, but a more modern interpretation, as with the two pillars in the High Priestess, is that black and white symbolize masculine/feminine, yang/yin and polarities or differences.

The Sphinx is a magical, mysterious creature, conjuring up images of Ancient Egypt and lost civilizations. Shakespeare, in *Love's Labours Lost*, describes love as "subtle as Sphinx" and we associate the Sphinx with someone who is inscrutable. The Charioteer is not just a sportsperson or a competitor. There is an element of the metaphysical, of hidden powers waiting to be tapped. As the master of the Sphinx, here is someone who is equally strong in body, mind, and spirit.

Links to Astrology

For me, the Chariot is most closely aligned with Mars, the planet of action, drive, and courage. Mars is also a powerful symbol for sport, especially those that display the skills of an individual rather than a team. At best he is Mars in his sign of exaltation, the earth sign of Capricorn, which shows that energy can be harnessed and channeled toward a specific goal or aim.

VIII

Strength

Here is a woman, calm and serene, mastering the open-mouthed lion with gentleness and apparent ease. Strength is shown as feminine power, not brute force.

STRENGTH

Traditional meaning
*Courage, fortitude,
patience.*

When this card appears in a reading it usually points to the need for patience and courage. A problem or a difficult situation can be tamed and overcome if you have the guts to tackle it and to remain steadfast in the face of adversity. It may be a question of being strong for someone else, or for yourself, which can include taming or restraining your feelings. Longing or frustration must be contained and endured, so this card is not for the faint-hearted or feeble-minded.

You can get what you want but not without acquiring emotional maturity, which means having to pass some kind of endurance test. Ranting and raving, feeling hard done by, or giving in to self-pity will get you nowhere. That which is desired requires patience, and that which needs to be endured must be borne with quiet confidence and good grace. Often there is a theme of having to stick to your guns or having to stand up for yourself, of having to walk into the lion's den with nothing but your own inner strength and convictions to protect you.

As a character there are similarities with the Queen of Wands, as both of these cards carry the lion symbolism of Leo. However, the Queen of Wands assumes a central role because she is naturally efficient and confident, whereas the Strength card shows that you are meeting the demands of a particular situation and are needing to call on your deepest inner resources for a reason.

At a more physical level this card can symbolize vitality. It is an encouraging card to see if you are dealing with health questions, as it suggests good recuperative powers and getting back to fitness in the fullness of time.

If the Strength card is flanked by difficult cards, we may need to ask if power is being misused or misapplied. There may be a message about needing to let go, knowing when to relinquish control, and admitting defeat rather than waiting for something that will never be.

Strength came up as the seventh card—where you will find yourself—in the Celtic Cross in a spread for a man who was desperately trying to come to terms with the fact that his wife had had an affair. She regretted it bitterly, and was doing everything she could to make it up to him, but to no avail. He felt so sick and betrayed that he had made himself ill and, although the affair was over, he was still torturing himself, especially with the fear that his marriage would not be able to recover and that he would end up losing her.

In this case the last two cards of the spread were so positive—the Nine of Cups (contentment) and the Wheel of Fortune as the outcome—that I had no hesitation in assuring him that he was not heading for the divorce courts. However, the road to forgiveness was going to be long and arduous and there was a lot of work to be done. Reconciliation was clearly on the horizon but it was a process that could not be rushed.

I concentrated on the Strength card as I felt that this pointed to the necessary effort and patience on both sides. There were no short cuts, nobody was going to wave a magic wand and make everything better, but even in the middle of a raging battle we have to try and concentrate on what we want the outcome to be. I tried to convey the message that only he could tame the beasts of anger and jealousy that were keeping him awake at night, and only he could find the strength to let it all go. Raging and cursing is easy. Finding the inner strength to confront and resolve a painful situation, especially when acknowledging our own part in it, is much harder. Fortunately, even though he was still agonizing, he acknowledged this to be true.

Interpreting Strength

One look at this card tells you that we are not dealing with physical strength. This picture represents not the strength of brute force or muscle power, but feminine power at its most effective. Strength is depicted as a skillful combination of firmness and kindness, as brain rather than brawn, and also as fearlessness. In some Tarot packs this card is called Fortitude.

Only two figures in the Tarot carry the symbol of infinity above their heads, the other one being the Magician, and this reinforces the sense that the woman's courage springs from a deep wisdom and that she carries the secrets of life.

Links to Astrology

The lion is the central symbol of the Strength card and there is a clear correlation with Leo. When this card appears I have often found there to be a Leo person at the center of a situation—proud, courageous, big-hearted, and capable.

Leo is ruled by the Sun, the symbol of life and wholeness. This reinforces the psychological message of the Strength card, which is to curb our more primitive impulses and to wrestle with our shadow side in order to develop strength of character.

IX the **Hermit**

THE HERMIT

Traditional meaning
Withdrawal,
contemplation, inner
counsel.

In many ways the Hermit represents our first real challenge in life's journey. All the other cards we have looked at so far have depicted magical, colorful, powerful, or heroic characters. In stark contrast, the Hermit is old, gray, and somber, halting us in our tracks, bringing us back down to earth and back into ourselves.

The Hermit card points to looking inside yourself for the answers, rather than looking to other people. Peace and quiet is required for any kind of contemplation, whether this is time out, deep soul-searching, existential angst, or just gathering your thoughts or licking your wounds after a difficult or upsetting experience. Either way, you need to find the right path toward understanding, which is crucial for your personal and spiritual development. This is not a modern-day concept. It was Socrates who said that the unexamined life is not worth living. But in the 21st century, many of us find ourselves under increasing pressure "to have" rather than "to be." Thus the quest for meaning and calming of the spirit has never been so important.

The Hermit is a gray, dismal card, evoking sadness, bleakness, and feelings of isolation. It is an existential truth that ultimately we are alone, a truth which many of us find hard to bear to the extent that we disbelieve or disregard it. Most of us are convinced that our happiness is to be found in another, not in ourselves, so the Hermit may appear when someone is dealing with the pain of their aloneness.

If this is the case the message is to try and stay connected with those around you, even if there isn't a special person. Learning to be self-sufficient and self-reliant can be a valuable lesson of the Hermit, but cutting off from friends, colleagues, or family can be detrimental, even dangerous, especially for someone who is depressed. Most of us are not capable of the kind of retreat that the Hermit card may at first suggest.

Often the Hermit card indicates a period of loneliness, so it is important to look at how you are spending your time

Links to Astrology
In planetary terms the Hermit correlates most closely with the symbolism of Saturn.

Saturn's colors are black and gray and he rules everything to do with time, whether this is learning to wait, coping with situations that are stuck, or facing up to the aging process and accepting our own mortality. Saturn also rules boundaries as well as barriers, echoing the theme of how we can connect or disconnect from the people around us. Saturn is also Father Time, symbolizing death and endings of all kinds.

alone. Meditation and contemplation can take different forms and do not necessarily require sitting in solitude. There is also a place for quiet walking, reading, writing, and so on. It is a time for finding things that are thought-provoking, inspiring, or which take you to a peaceful place. Time alone needs to be therapeutic and solitude can be a completely different experience from loneliness.

When the Hermit card appears in a spread it can also mean that retreat is better than attack. It is unwise to force issues or to put pressure on yourself or on someone else. In fact, someone may withdraw even further from you if you try to push them. Or it may be the other way around, that you need to distance yourself from someone who is negative or problematic in some way. Either way, this is a card of time and space. Someone or something just cannot be rushed.

Finally, the Hermit card may appear for someone who has been bereaved and who is shrouded in grief. This is the ultimate aloneness, one that has to be endured and for which there is no remedy except time.

The Hermit appeared as the card for the present moment for a woman in her late thirties. It was preceded by the Five of Pentacles (poverty) and she confirmed that she had just been through the worst financial difficulties of her life. This was due to having supported her husband while he started his own business. The business, however, did not take off and collapsed, by which time they were considering bankruptcy. This had put an enormous strain on their relatively new marriage, but she assured me that they both still wanted it to work.

However, getting the marriage to work was another matter. As I talked about the nature of the Hermit card, she told me that it sounded very familiar, as her husband had withdrawn from her and she was finding it impossible to talk to him. It was the proverbial "brick wall" and she was contemplating a trial separation.

Fortunately, the outcome card was excellent. The Two of Cups (union) suggested that they would reunite, albeit not immediately. The outcome card related to six months hence and a quick look in the Ephemeris (daily astrological data) showed me that she was experiencing Saturn transits, and that these would be coming to an end in six months time. I encouraged her to hang on in there. In the meantime, the Hermit card painted an accurate picture from all angles—his withdrawal, her isolation, and the loneliness of the marriage. I felt that a trial separation was somewhat drastic but that some time apart would certainly be beneficial.

X

Wheel of Fortune

WHEEL OF FORTUNE

Traditional Meaning
Change, cycles of life.

Links to Astrology
The Wheel of Fortune correlates with the symbolism of Jupiter, the planet of luck and opportunity.

After the cheerless encounter with the Hermit, the Wheel of Fortune comes as a relief. There are more difficult cards to come, but for now the Wheel of Fortune is turning in your favor, heralding the start of a new cycle and moving you towards your destiny.

The Wheel of Fortune is a magical card. It connects you with that which is greater than you are, a benign cosmos that assists you and teaches you. The gods are smiling on you and everything is going your way, so the Wheel of Fortune is a welcome sight in any reading.

However, I have found that this card is not always about good luck. The mythical creatures surrounding the wheel are each studying a book, pointing to the theme of knowledge. There is a sense of progress that has come through the active acquisition of knowledge, and the resulting wisdom is the fruit of past or present labors. In this way the Wheel of Fortune suggests that you have successfully sought out, or are seeking out, your good fortune through learning valuable lessons and that you are now on the right track. This is not just about a stroke of luck, but a "lucky" break can now make all the difference and put you on a roll. The wheel always turns full circle, and although we tend to use this phrase in terms of retribution, it also applies to reaping your rewards. In this sense the Wheel of Fortune is like your good karma.

The image of the wheel is loaded with this kind of symbolism—cycles, infinity, reincarnation, wholeness, progress, perpetuity—so each turn of the wheel is a new start, a turn for the better and also a completion of some kind.

JUPITER AND THE PATH OF GOOD FORTUNE

The Wheel of Fortune correlates with the symbolism of Jupiter, the planet of luck and opportunity. This emphasizes the stark contrast of this card with the Hermit. The Hermit equates to Saturn, a planet known as the Greater malefic in traditional terms, whereas the Wheel of Fortune equates with Jupiter, known as the Greater benefic.

These two planets follow each other in the astrological hierarchy and symbolize opposite principles, illustrated by the fact that Saturn is dignified (strong) in Capricorn, Jupiter's sign of detriment, and in detriment (weak) in Cancer, Jupiter's sign of exaltation. Whereas Saturn limits and restricts, Jupiter signals expansion and opportunity, ruling everything to do with travel, education, wisdom, liberation, and justice. Anything that can broaden your outlook or widen your horizons, either mentally or physically, is Jupiterian in nature and the Wheel of Fortune carries the same symbolism.

Jupiter rules fiery Sagittarius, the sign of the traveler and the higher mind. Sagittarians are often spoken of as lucky people and "Jupiter luck" is that apparent

last minute twist of fate that rescues someone from difficulty at the eleventh hour. Although this kind of luck undoubtedly exists, there is also an argument that such people actually play a part in creating their own luck, either through past efforts or some kind of act of faith, which invariably turns out to be justified and invites good fortune in.

The Wheel of Fortune can often be seen as your good karma or reaping your rewards.

Interpreting the Wheel of Fortune

We have reached the halfway point of the journey and, as with the World, the last card of the Major Arcana, this card carries images of the four fixed signs of the zodiac in each corner—a woman for Aquarius, the eagle for Scorpio, the bull for Taurus, and the lion for Leo. This time they are all winged, portrayed as mythical or hybrid figures. Again, as in the Chariot, the sphinx is the central figure, this time perched on top of the wheel and armed with a sword. The wheel is being carried on the back of a griffin.

XI

Justice

A regal figure of a woman sits on a throne, her red robes adorned with a golden cloak. She sits between two pillars so, like the High Priestess, she can be seen as a uniting force. She carries a sword in one hand, symbolizing the need for truth, and a pair of scales in the other, representing the need for balance and fairness.

JUSTICE

Traditional meaning
Decisions, legal affairs.

When the Justice card appears in a spread it indicates the need to stand back, to weigh up the pros and cons, and to look at a situation from different angles. Quite often there is a significant and specific decision looming, or it may just be that you need to understand something from another's point of view. Either way, there are always two sides to every story and you need to apprise yourself of all the facts rather than jumping to conclusions.

The Justice card can also mean that there are legal affairs to be dealt with. If there is a matter going to court then the supporting cards in the spread will indicate whether or not a verdict will go in your favor. It can also indicate a situation in which you need to know your rights and you may need to seek out legal advice.

The appearance of the Justice card can also point to the value of a third person. Whether there are actual legal concerns on hand, or whether the issue involves a personal decision or situation, some kind of arbitrator can be an enormous help. In a professional capacity this could be a solicitor, a barrister, or any organization that offers help and advice.

In a personal context the Justice card indicates an objective outsider, a disinterested third party, or someone you can trust to be unbiased. Often a situation can only be seen for what it really is if you take out the emotion, cool it down, and look at the facts. This is not always easy or possible for the person who is deeply involved, but someone else on the outside can see the things you can't and enable negotiation. Or you may be the one who needs to fulfill the role of arbitrator. Either way, that which is fair, rational, and reasonable must triumph over personal feelings or desires, no matter how passionate these might be. You may also have to tolerate ambiguity rather than insisting on a right or wrong outcome.

MARS IN LIBRA

At a universal level Mars is the planet of drive, energy, and initiative. In psychological astrology he speaks of our anger and how we express it, how we go to war, how we push and shove—or not. Thus Mars is at home in single minded, ego orientated Aries or determined, powerful Scorpio. His nature is clearly in conflict with the more passive, vacillating nature of lazy Libra, a sign known for indecisiveness and fear of confrontation.

However, in terms of the Justice card, Mars in Libra is an excellent astrological analogy

as it encapsulates the passive/active polarity inherent in the card—thought-provoking arguments that are assertive rather than aggressive. There is the intelligence to think something through and the guts to stand up and be counted.

Also Libra is the natural arbitrator of the zodiac as it rules the seventh house of the horoscope, the house of partnership and the concerns of any significant other. The legendary inability of Librans to make up their minds stems from the fact that they can always see every point of view. A typical Libran loves to collect different opinions and mull them all over and may even play devil's advocate just to encourage debate.

JUPITER AND THE NINTH HOUSE

In the horoscope justice and all things legal belong to the domain of the ninth house. This is the house of Sagittarius, the sign of the traveler and truth seeker, and it is often referred to as the house of the higher mind. Philosophy, education, religion, and the acquisition of knowledge all belong to the ninth house and it is ruled by Jupiter, known as the Greater Benefic. This reminds us that true justice can be achieved only if it is married to wisdom, compassion, and humanity.

Interpreting Justice

Whereas the High Priestess invites us into the mysterious realms of the metaphysical, the Justice card symbolizes the intellectual skills of reason, thought, and deliberation within the human world, the capacity for which is crucial to every civilized society.

Interestingly, Justice is represented by a female figure yet she embodies the so-called masculine function of head over heart. She is the only figure of the Major Arcana to carry a sword, symbolizing the fight for truth, contrasting with the scales in her other hand, which speak of the need for balance and fairness. She is, then, a combination of masculine and feminine, active and passive, warrior and judge. She upholds the need for tough logic rather than sentiment and asks that feelings be tempered with objectivity.

Links to Astrology

The Sword in one hand corresponds with both the element of air and the planet Mars—the god of war—while the scales in the other represent the air sign of Libra. In traditional astrology the combination of Mars in Libra is not a happy one as this is said to be Mars' sign of detriment, ie weakness.

the **Hanged Man**

THE HANGED MAN

Traditional meaning
Sacrifice, deeper
understanding.

Once we become acquainted with this card we realize that the only frightening thing about it is its name. Whenever this card appears I point out that the figure is not hanging by his neck but is suspended by his ankle and is neither dead nor wounded. In fact, the upside down, haloed figure is alive and in no hurry to struggle free. Neither is he in any discomfort as he crosses his other leg and his arms behind him and quietly contemplates the world from his own angle.

There is an element of surrender here, as life may not be panning out the way we think it is supposed to but, for now, there is nothing that we can do about it. The solutions do not lie in action but in thought and contemplation. When this card appears it may seem that our lives are upside down and everything is back to front. We may even be in a situation in which we feel trapped and helpless. But by mulling something over and looking at it from a new angle, our perspective shifts and we can see what is wrong.

This is where the traditional meaning of sacrifice enters, as a new perspective brings new understanding. It is time to sweep all the deadwood out of our lives and unburden ourselves of the things that are holding us back, whether these may be a job, a relationship, a lifestyle, or an ingrained belief.

We may need to rid ourselves of "I can't" or "I could never" as, although saying goodbye to something may be a wrench, we finally know in our heart of hearts that it is the only way forward. We

The Hanged Man came up for a woman who had for many years enjoyed her single life in London. Life had changed dramatically as she had met her current partner and their first child was six months old. The next step was to move to the country and she acknowledged a certain resistance to saying goodbye to her old life and embracing the new. The Hanged Man spoke perfectly of her need to find a new perspective, to leave her single life behind and to adopt her new role and image in a positive way. She felt that this move was a stepping stone to a better quality of life but, in the first instance, it was a case of accepting a different life and making all the adjustments this involved.

may realize that our inertia is a form of resistance. Any sacrifices are made in the spirit of improving our lives in the long term, even though we may be struggling in the short term.

The Hanged Man can be seen as a card of death and rebirth, as it symbolizes change involving a sense of loss or disorientation. It is also a card of adjustment as we adapt to new circumstances and rethink our lives and our beliefs. It is a card of maturity and growing up. We are also reminded that our thoughts can be a powerful factor in shaping the outer world.

SATURN

There is no getting away from the fact that Saturn is a heavy planet and Saturn transits or progressions nearly always point to hard times. However, these times are not without value and, when linking the symbolism of the Hanged Man with this planet, we are reminded that learning tough lessons puts us on the road to deeper understanding. The Hermit card may point to the misery and isolation imposed by Saturn at his worst, but the correlation with the Hanged Man reminds us of the potential depth of the Saturnian experience. As psychological astrologer Liz Greene writes:

> "Saturn...is not merely a representative of pain, restriction, and discipline; he is also a symbol of the psychic process,...by which an individual may utilize the experiences of pain, restriction, and discipline...for greater...fulfillment." [9]

Interpreting the Hanged Man

This is a picture of suspended animation. This kind of immobility is difficult for most of us, especially if we are naturally busy and can't bear to "hang around" for developments. But the message is that time out doesn't have to be an ordeal. As with the High Priestess and the Hermit, we are being urged into stillness, to slow down and to look within. If we can find this serenity, we will find it much easier to reach acceptance, whether this is of a situation or of another person.

Links to Astrology

As with the Hermit, the Hanged Man correlates most closely with the symbolism of Saturn, the planet of work, effort, and restriction. However, it also rules everything to do with time, so when Saturn comes into the picture we find that life is harder work than usual, that we have to wait for what we want and that there are no short cuts. For this reason he has earned the reputation of being the spoilsport of the zodiac.

There is also a case for linking the Hanged Man with Neptune, as this planet is the co-ruler of Pisces, the sign that rules the 12th house of the horoscope. In traditional astrology this is the house of sacrifice and suffering that ultimately leads to redemption.

XIII

Death

When this card appears in a reading the sight of the skeleton clad in black armor is indeed a chilling figure and it is up to the reader to dispel reactions of fear and panic as quickly as possible. If I turn over the Death card I immediately comment, "Don't panic at the sight of the Death card. We'll talk about what it really means as we go along."

DEATH

Traditional meaning
Change, rebirth

Here it is, the card that everyone dreads. The Death card is largely responsible for the fear that the Tarot can provoke, either because it breeds the mistaken idea of links with the occult or because it confronts our terror of our own mortality. In most societies death is still the biggest taboo, the biggest fact of life that we are all expert at ignoring.

So what does this card mean? Firstly, it very rarely signifies actual death.

Throughout 15 years of readings I remember only three examples of the Death card relating to bereavement, one of which was to a past bereavement and the other two to people already terminally ill. In one reading a man told me that he wanted to know when he was going to die, to which I replied that I am not in the business of predicting death.

As always, think symbolically. The Death card is telling us that something is "dead," or on its way out. Whether it be a situation, a relationship, a job, or a way of life, something has had its day and is coming to an end. As painful as this may be, nothing new can come about until the old life has decayed and disappeared, clearing the way for new growth. For this reason the changes that are symbolized by the Death card are often profound and permanent.

For the Tarot reader this is a challenging card. It is too easy to glamorize the Death card and to dress it up as "change and transformation." It sounds much better like that. However this misses the point that some changes are not easy or swift but in fact quite the opposite. The Death card points to events that are frightening, painful, and traumatic, and that bring loss, grief, despair, or deep regret. Big changes for the better may be the eventual outcome but it is usually some time before we can look back and say that terrible time was the best thing that ever happened to me. That lies in the future. In the present moment it feels as if the world is falling in and life is over. The truth is that life as we knew it is over and the clouds may be far too black and ominous for us to see the silver linings just yet.

The Death card can also symbolize absence and feeling so lost and apart from someone that they feel dead to us.

PLUTO AND THE EIGHTH HOUSE

Time and time again you will read that Pluto is about "change and transformation" but these keywords fall short of describing the Plutonic experience. As American astrologer Caroline Casey so accurately writes, "*When*

Pluto is our travel agent, our ticket to heaven includes a stopover in hell." [10] Pluto rules invisibility and nothingness and his first act is to annihilate our sense of self and to strip away that which is comfortable or safe. The solid foundations of our lives turn to quicksand as we come face to face with loss, grief, obsession, disintegration, depression, or desperation. We find ourselves traveling through our own underworld and the journey is a trip to hell and back.

That's the bad news. The good news is that it is, eventually, a journey that can teach us more about life and about ourselves than any other. *"Pluto brings us to our knees, forcing us to surrender to full feeling."* [11] No longer can we skate happily along the surface. Having been to the edge and looked over we realize that Pluto or the Death card symbolize the process of change during which we learn the resilience of the human spirit and the art of survival.

In the words of Almustafa in *The Prophet*:

"You would know the secret of death. But how shall you find it unless you seek it in the heart of life?" [12]

So we do the things we thought we could never do and survive the things we thought we could never survive. Only then do we reach rebirth and transformation of the phoenix rising from the ashes. Only having experienced powerlessness can we start to regain control.

Links to Astrology
In the horoscope death belongs to the domain of the eighth house, ruled by the sign of Scorpio—which probably explains why Scorpio often gets bad press. Scorpio is traditionally ruled by Mars but is co-ruled by Pluto, who is the god of the underworld in mythology. It is not uncommon for people to be experiencing Pluto transits if the Death card comes up, and understanding the nature of this planet is helpful when interpreting the Death card.

The Death card appeared in a reading where it related to a past bereavement and this reading has always stuck in my mind. The reading was for a man in his fifties and the Death card was at the bottom of the spread, relating to the past. Generally I find that it relates to the previous 12 months, but he said immediately that it referred to a few years ago when he had lost his 18-year-old daughter. His sadness was still palpable but his courage was amazing.

In the aftermath of her death he too had "died" in a sense. He realized that he had not been living his own life to its full potential. He completely reevaluated his values and priorities and found that he could no longer continue in a nine-to-five job that meant nothing to him. He quit and began nursing mentally disabled children, in which he found his true vocation. Although nothing could ever replace his daughter, he said that he saw his work as her bequest to him, how he owed it to her to live his life to the full, and how his life had changed beyond all recognition due to her death.

XIV Temperance

TEMPERANCE

Traditional meaning
Balance, moderation

The theme of relief or reward after darkness is first seen in the Wheel of Fortune following the bleakness of the Hermit card, and again in the Star after the shock of the Tower. At this stage of the journey, the serenity of the Temperance card releases us from the pain and fear of Death, redresses the balance and provides a welcome watershed before the encounter with the Devil.

Temperance paints a picture of beauty, peace, and comfort. A haloed, golden-haired angel, robed in the purity of white, stands at a lakeside. On one side of her grow beautiful flowers, while on the other a path cuts its way through meadow land and up into the mountains towards a rising sun—symbolizing dawning consciousness and coming back to life. The angel wears enormous wings and she holds two cups, pouring an apparently continuous stream of water from one into the other. After the dark desert of Death we emerge thirsty for life and this powerful image of light and replenishment is a major stepping stone on the road to rebirth.

The word "temperance" may at first conjure up the idea of sobriety. The Temperance card, however, is not about abstinence but about moderation, "*the practice or habit of restraining oneself in provocation, passion, desire.*" [13] It is one of the four cardinal virtues, the others being justice, prudence, and fortitude.

When Temperance appears in a reading the first requirement is patience. This is a card of assessment, thought, and calmness. It is no good reaching for the unreachable star or rushing recklessly in pursuit of the unattainable. Passion will only get us so far before we run out of steam and drop back down to earth. We need to stop and look at the options—which may mean inaction:

> "*This card means right action, doing the correct thing in whatever situation arises. Very often this means doing nothing. The intemperate person always needs to be doing something, but very often a situation requires a person to simply wait.*" [14]

Links to Astrology
This card is often assigned to the fire sign of Sagittarius or its ruler, Jupiter. However, Temperance is not really a card of action or expansion, but a card of balance. In this sense it is, like Justice, a Libran card—the sign of the scales. It is also an earth/water card which fits the symbolism of Taurus (fixed earth), depicted in the rural landscape, along with Pisces (mutable water), as illustrated by the lake and the stream of water between the two cups.

The other important message of Temperance is compromise, equilibrium, and emotional maturity. The Cups correspond to the element of water, which correlates to our emotional life, and the pouring of the water from cup to cup illustrates staying in touch with feelings on both sides and going with the flow. We will not get what we want if we impose our own ideas or desires on another, or if we look for perfection. We need to find the rhythm of a situation, a relationship, another individual, and dance to the same drum.

RELATIONSHIPS

If the Temperance card appears with regard to a relationship it speaks of hope, promise, and enormous potential. However, this is not love through rose-tinted spectacles. Because Temperance is primarily concerned with matters of balance, it is an excellent card for any partnership issue. A mutual desire for connection and learning each other's language provides fertile ground for love to grow and flourish.

SITUATIONS

In relation to a specific situation, Temperance advises us to find the middle line and not to take sides. There is a need to give equal weight to all factors or all others involved. As with the Justice card, personal agendas need to be sidelined for the good of the whole. We may also have to play the role of arbitrator.

Interpreting Temperance

The most important symbolic detail of the Temperance card lies in the angel's feet as, once again, we meet imagery that promotes the harmonizing of opposites. She has one foot on the grass (being earthed, grounded) and the other in the water (the emotions). It is this perfectly balanced combination of practicality and feeling that really matters, the awareness of consciousness and the unconscious as two sides of the same coin. If we sacrifice one for the other, we suppress a vital function and become incomplete, one-sided, and uncreative.

Temperance is an excellent card to see regarding issues concerning relationships, indicating equilibrium and emotional maturity.

the **Devil**

THE DEVIL

Traditional meaning
*Bondage, base
instincts, bad habits*

The Death card is generally regarded as the most terrifying card in the pack but the Devil can also strike horror into the heart of your client. Undoubtedly, he presents a frightening picture with his horned animal's head, bat's wings, and clawed feet, squatting over a man and woman who are naked, horned, and chained together. He evokes the stuff of nightmares and visions of purgatory.

Venturing into the ground of difficult feelings will usually quickly establish if a painful relationship is the issue. Whatever the story, there is no getting away from the fact that the Devil card is a huge warning and is flagging up that there is something horribly wrong. I have seen this card show innumerable times for affairs, horrendous triangular setups that are capable of bringing out the primitive in all of us. Whether it is the role of the spurned lover, the one who is being left, or the one who is doing the leaving, most of us will fight tooth and claw when pushed to the edge with emotions rubbed raw. Anyone who has been through an acrimonious or messy divorce, for example, will bear witness to how quickly the superficial veneer of sophistication and manners can be stripped away.

I have also seen this card show more than once for someone who is tempted to have an affair or who has developed an overwhelming crush, but any questions about pursuing a love interest when the Devil is present simply have to be negated. The answer is no. The Devil warns us that we are playing with fire, inviting situations which will be trouble and which could destroy us. We must question our motivation or the motives of another, and accept that things are not as they seem.

I have also seen the Devil card show up for addiction, such as alcoholism, which can turn an otherwise lovely person into an abusive monster. In one reading the Devil card was a woman's son, who was institutionalized for drug abuse, diagnosed as paranoid, and facing years of treatment. In such situations the damage is done and the reality has to be faced and dealt with. But in a situation where there is still a choice the message of the Devil card is to get out and don't look back. If someone is hellbent on any course of action symbolized by the Devil, it will come with a heavy price tag.

Links to Astrology

The Devil is aptly echoed by Pluto, the co-ruler of Scorpio. All that is dark, destructive, or obsessive is Plutonic. With this planet we experience big changes, mostly characterized by loss, pain, cruelty, or fear. Life becomes like a nightmare and our resources are tested to the limit.

The themes of the Devil card are even more powerfully reflected in the combination of Pluto with Venus. Here is the stuff of Fatal Attraction—the torments of unrequited love, unsatiated lust, desperate neediness, loneliness, and obsession at its worst.

Interpreting the Devil

While I do not believe in playing down uncomfortable images, I am quick to allay feelings of terror or panic. Such feelings are not helpful for the client or the reader. There is cause for concern when this card shows but it is generally not about being claimed by the forces of evil! In the modern-day world the Devil card mostly points to obsession, and this is often played out through an unhealthy or destructive relationship. Drawing a parallel with the Lovers card can be useful as this card also shows a couple standing side by side, but it is an image of light and love with a heavenly angel blessing the union. By comparison, the Devil card is dark and sinister, symbolizing jealousy, control, addiction, abuse, cruelty, or the manipulation of another to serve our own needs.

The Devil appeared in a reading with a woman I knew quite well. I also knew her to be happily married, so the Devil card was a shock. With a great deal of trepidation I took the Devil by the horns and went in and, as I spoke of this card, I was amazed to see the knowing smile on her face and the intense nods of agreement.

I finally asked if she knew of someone who was obsessed with her and the answer was a resounding yes. It was not another man but a woman of the same age. She didn't believe that the woman's motivation was sexual—although the lustful connotations of the Devil made this a question—but that it seemed to be more a case of over-identification.

To cut a long story short, the woman in question had increasingly and insidiously encroached upon her friend's life and any attempt to escape her unwanted company was futile. The good thing that came out of the reading was that my client had temporarily lost sight of how unhealthy and destructive this situation really was. I reminded her that she could still put up some boundaries and that she didn't have to over-sympathize or feel responsible. She readily acknowledged that a large part of her resignation was due to feeling powerless in this situation. I urged her to take some power back and, at a later date, she told me that matters were not resolved but much improved once she had decided to be less accommodating.

the **Tower**

THE TOWER

A concrete tower sits atop a craggy mountain, reaching up into the clouds, and a bolt of lightning strikes from above. Flames leap from the windows, while two figures are in terrified freefall, their only possible means of escape being to plummet into the unknown darkness below.

Traditional meaning
The shattering of old structures

As with Death and the Devil, this is one of the most visually alarming cards of the Tarot. The first thing to point out to a client is that the Tower doesn't spell destruction at the physical level. The Tower is first and foremost a metaphor for the structure of the life we have built for ourselves. Every experience that has shaped us and made us who we are, all our beliefs, opinions, and attitudes, are cemented into this structure and dictate the rules and patterns by which we now live. The irony is that this apparent security can all too easily become our prison and the choices we have made our jailers.

Without a context it is impossible to predict what the Tower might mean because the Tower takes us into the realm of the unpredictable. All we can expect is the unexpected. If this card appears in a spread for a specific question, such as a job

or a relationship, then the best that can be said is that matters will not go smoothly. On the contrary, even the best laid plans and intentions are likely to be dramatically overturned and a situation can end up being out of control, or at least out of our control. A promised job may be offered to a rival, the company may go bankrupt, a partner may dump us unceremoniously for someone else without warning, or we may hear news which shocks or upsets us.

In terms of our inner world the Tower speaks of those times that stop us in our tracks and turn us upside down. Like the figures in the card we may go into some kind of freefall, losing our sense of direction and trying to fight off the demons of rage, anxiety, or panic. The catalyst can be anything but the result is the same—the shocking realization that we are not the person we thought we were, or that we are not invulnerable, and that the things that happen to other people can happen to us. Internalized images of our world, ourselves, another person, disintegrate and, no matter how carefully we may try to reconstruct, things are never going to be the same again.

At this point there is a choice. In the face of calamity we can either crumble and fall apart, or we sweep up the rubble, get over the shock and throw our old scripts

Links to Astrology
Uranus is the planet of rebellion, revolution, and unexpected changes. People with strong Uranian themes are unconventional, unusual, and brilliant. However, they can also be unstable and prone to mental illness.

away. This is not easy to do, but there is no point in clinging to the ruins of a life under a demolition order.

URANUS AND THE MID-LIFE CRISIS

Fittingly, Uranus has an erratic orbit and travels around the zodiac every 76–84 years. This means that he reaches his half-way point anywhere between the 38th and 42nd birthday, a contact, which is called the Uranus Half Return. In psychological astrology this corresponds to the mid-life crisis, when we become acutely conscious of the passage of time and start to question what it's all about. The things we have always accepted come up for scrutiny and we rebel against Saturn, the preceding planet in the astrological hierarchy. Saturn plays by the rules, Uranus breaks them. Saturn is the work ethic, sensible and structured, but Uranus explodes the boundaries and throws caution to the winds.

The Uranus Half Return is when we do the things we've never done because it's now or never. Those who are married to the wrong person leave; those who are unmarried fall in love and tie the knot; women who have never had children suddenly get pregnant, or a "last chance" baby is conceived; those who have labored for years in a boring job quit and go walking in the Himalayas; and those who have gadded about take up a career.

In effect, Uranus and the Tower bring the same message home. In the interests of our personal development, quest for happiness, and spiritual growth, that which is redundant has to go, and that part of us which has lain dormant must come to life.

Interpreting the Tower

When the Tower appears in a spread it indicates that huge change is in the air, usually in the shape of a bolt from the blue, something that pulls the rug out from under our feet. In our outer world the Tower symbolizes the unforeseen event that throws a spanner in the works.

The Tower often symbolizes great change or taking a leap into the unknown.

the **Star**

THE STAR

The Star card comes as a relief and a joy. The preceding two cards, the Devil and the Tower, have taken us into the realms of all that is unconscious, uncontrollable, or destructive. The Star symbolizes the world in the morning after the storm, taking us back into the sparkling daylight where everything is washed clean and visibility is restored.

This is a wonderful card for getting in touch with our bodies and reclaiming our libido in a healthy way. Gone are the tortured, desperate appetites of the Devil. Our sexuality is now a natural part of our humanity and sense of wholeness. So when the Star appears in a reading it can point to an improved sex life or a new lover, especially someone who knows how to put us in touch with our true needs.

The Star reminds us of the importance of feeling good about ourselves and enjoying a positive body image. The water tumbling from the pitchers is also a symbol of life itself, so this card points to good health and extra vitality. This is one of the best cards to see if you are dealing with questions of health or fertility as it promises full recovery or conception. In fact, if someone is asking about children,

Traditional meaning
Renewal,
rejuvenation.

The Star is generally a wonderful card to see in a spread, especially in questions about love, relationships, and sexuality. I remember one woman in her late fifties telling me that she had come to terms with her aging body through massage and aromatherapy, and I applauded her decision that saggy didn't have to mean unsexy.

But remember that any card in conflict with the more difficult cards reveals its themes as a source of crisis. In a reading for a woman whose marriage was seemingly on the rocks the Star crossed the Hermit in the center of the Celtic Cross. As the Hermit signals retreat or aloneness it is virtually opposite in meaning to the Star, which is ultimately about being connected to the forces of life at both a physical and spiritual level. I ventured into intimate territory and she confirmed that their sex life had ground to a halt. The lack of physical intimacy reinforced the failing emotional closeness and was making her unutterably miserable.

She didn't know how to stop the rot and, without the togetherness and contact symbolized by the Star, she could see no way out of the Hermit state. As the reading progressed it became apparent that some kind of counseling would help, as there were numerous issues, which needed to be cleared out of the way.

the appearance of the Star may mean that she is already pregnant.

One of the most delightful things about symbolism is the art of interpreting physical impossibilities. The Star is a good example, as the card depicts a daytime scene with the stars clearly visible in the blue sky. This reminds us that the stars are always there even though we may not be able to see them and the same message is true of so many things in life. Just because something is not staring us in the face it doesn't mean that it's not there.

In a reading the Star points to a positive outcome. It is a card of good fortune and rejuvenation, so complications become simplified, depression is on its way out, and it's good to be alive.

Interpreting the Star

The Star is a beautiful card, mostly because of its simplicity. The naked female figure kneels on the grass by a lake and, with a pitcher in each hand, she pours water on to the ground and back into the lake. This is a picture of replenishment, playfulness, going back to nature, and being in harmony with our environment. The maiden emanates contentment, reminding us that true happiness does not come from material possessions or from other people. Her peace and serenity come from within as she plays happily alone.

As a powerful image of rebirth her lack of self-consciousness is also important. Body and spirit are as one and there is nothing to hide, fear, or repress. The element of water symbolizes our emotions and in the Star we can revert back to the innocence of childhood where feelings flow and shame is an unknown experience.

Links to Astrology

The central symbolism of the Star card is flowing water, hence you will see analogies with Aquarius, the sign of the water bearer. However, Aquarius is actually an air sign, so I prefer to liken the Star to Pisces, the sign of mutable water. Pisces is one of the most fertile and instinctive of the signs and is co-ruled by mystical Neptune, god of the sea and planet of dreams. The Star is also like Venus in Pisces, Venus' strongest sign.

The flowing water shown in the Star card often symbolizes health and extra vitality.

XVIII | the **Moon**

THE MOON

Traditional meaning
Change, uncertainty.

The Moon is a powerful symbol of womankind, feminine energy, and fertility. Her orbit tracks the 28 days of the menstrual cycle and her waxing and waning symbolizes the pattern of conception, pregnancy, and birth. By contrast, masculine or solar power is fixed and linear, as the Sun never changes its shape. But just as the Moon apparently changes shape every night, so are women hormonal and changeable in their feelings and moods.

In this card we see the three phases of the Moon—new, half moon, and full—represented in one orb, which in turn correlates with the three archetypal faces of the maiden, the mother, and the crone. There are also three Moon goddesses—Artemis for the New Moon, Demeter the earth mother for the Full Moon, and Hecate the witch for the Dark of the Moon—the three-day period of darkness before the appearance of the New Moon, which is associated with the occult.

The Moon rules the realm of the unconscious—feelings, needs, instincts, and responses—and it is this mysterious, shadowy world of the emotions that reflects the Moon's traditional divinatory meaning in the Tarot. When the Moon appears in a spread it points to a situation of change, fluctuation, uncertainty, or even illusion. Just as the New Moon is apparently a sliver but is in reality the only visible part of the whole picture, things are not necessarily as they seem and we need to question the image being presented.

"I know" is the voice of certainty, which springs from logic or reason in the face of that which is obvious. But with the Moon it is the "I *somehow* know" quality that counts as we tune in to the undercurrents and allow ourselves to be guided by our instincts and gut reactions. When the Moon represents a situation, nothing should be done in haste. We need to hold on to some healthy cynicism in the interests of self-protection while we are waiting to see what unfolds and develops.

In my own readings I have also found the Moon to indicate another woman in a triangular setup. Unfortunately, the negative side to feminine power can be manipulative, cunningly subtle, and tricky, and the Moon can indicate scenarios that are characterized by deceit and that can be incredibly complicated or painful.

Links to Astrology

The Moon has a multitude of meanings. She rules the water sign of Cancer, symbolizing home, family, protection, and security. She is the Lady of the Night and rules the world of women, the unconscious, receptivity, shadows, mirrors, and all that is habitual, instinctive, or changeable.

Everyone knows their own Sun sign, but do you know your Moon sign? Whether you are a man or a woman, the Moon describes your feminine side, your needs, instinctive reactions, and emotional responses.

Interpreting the Moon

At a universal level the Moon is loaded with her own symbolism. The crayfish clambering from the water symbolizes the unconscious, while the images of Hecate's animals, the dog and wolf baying at the Moon, tap us into Full Moon lunacy and witchery. The Moon's phases mark her pull on the tides and the wrong or right time for spells, sowing, and reaping. No magician or astrologer worth his or her salt would undertake any important matter without checking the activity of the Moon first. In horary astrology, which involves casting a chart for a question rather than the birth moment of an individual, the Moon's last and next aspect is the first thing to be noted and is crucial to judgment.

The Moon was the center card in the Relationship spread for a woman in her late twenties. She had been with her partner for 18 months and was very much in love with him, but she was uncertain about the future in spite of the fact that he was talking about marriage. The center card often speaks of the heart of the matter, the nub of the issue around which everything else revolves, so I focused on the Moon as the possible source of her uncertainty.

As I talked about the symbolism of this card, about illusion or deception, she nodded in agreement. I asked her if she knew of another woman and the answer was yes. She had felt for some time that things weren't quite right and, somewhat shamefacedly, she admitted that she had gone through his mail. Her worst fears were confirmed when she found a letter, which was not only a love letter but one that also contained a photograph of the other woman—holding their nine-month-old son.

Piecing things together it was evident that he had met my client just at the time that his other girlfriend had conceived. He had never mentioned this other relationship or referred to the existence of a child. The letter made no reference to his current girlfriend, so this other woman was in the dark too. This painful situation bore all the hallmarks of the Moon.

Amazingly, but encouragingly, the future cards of the relationship spread were excellent—the Two of Cups (union) and the Knight of Cups (suitor)—so I felt that his desire to marry her was genuine. She wanted to clear the air and, as she was a Sagittarian, the sign of truth, I agreed that it had to be the best way forward.

the **Sun**

XIX

THE SUN

A huge Sun streams down on a wall of sunflowers in full bloom and on a naked child sitting astride a horse. The child's arms are flung wide with joy, as if to embrace the gift of life and the promise of a golden future. The Moon has her phases and faces, but the Sun wears just one face and never changes shape. So here we emerge from the shadowy night world into the glorious light of day where life is obvious and uncomplicated.

The Sun is the ultimate symbol of life—the source of all creation—and is a wonderful card to see in any reading. At a physical level the Sun speaks of glowing health, vitality, and a sense of general well-being and is an excellent omen for any health questions. This card speaks of good mental health too so, at a psychological level, it is about feeling whole, positive, and centered.

In terms of representing any situation, event, or goal this card symbolizes

Traditional meaning
Success, well being.

The Sun card came up in a reading for a woman whose cards I had done three years previously. Often, modern day Tarot is not just about divination but also about providing counseling and assistance with problem-solving, which means that the majority of readings are sought because of life's problems, difficulties, and crises. However sometimes there is the pleasure of doing a reading for someone whose life is pretty much sorted out and going the way it should be.

Such a reading came up for this woman. When she arrived I noticed that she was looking exceptionally well—in fact, she was positively radiating good health and energy—and the Sun appeared as one of her past cards. I commented on how she was moving from a position of strength and success and she told me that she had recently been promoted at work. This had been an excellent move for her—she was the blue-eyed girl of the moment and she was loving it.

Her other past card was the Page of Cups, which often signals conception. I asked her if she and her partner were trying for a baby, and she confirmed that this was her second month off the contraceptive pill. With the Page of Cups being paired with the Sun I judged that she was either already pregnant or was about to be, and she did in fact conceive two weeks later. The Sun also repeated as the center card in a stunning relationship spread (and she is also a Leo).

undisputed success. The Sun is shining on us, we are in the spotlight and our moment of glory is at hand. Well-deserved praise or recognition is ours for the taking and there is a sense of belonging, of being in the right place at the right time.

The triumphal right place shown by the Sun is often about being at the center of things. Just as the Sun is the center of our solar system, the central body around which the other planets revolve, so the Sun can indicate that we are at the center of our own universe. This can manifest in our outer world, not only by one-off achievements, but also by finding our niche or our true vocation. In terms of our inner world the Sun symbolizes that all too elusive prize of human happiness. It is an excellent card to see in a relationship spread as it shows that emotionally we are in a space of light, love, and warmth. We are wanted, prized, and valued and we sit at the heart of our partner's world.

LEO

In astrology the Sun rules the fire sign of Leo. Think of the Leo people you know and you will probably recognize straight away how much they seek out and thrive on situations in which they can take center stage. Give a Leo an audience and make them feel special and they couldn't be happier. Alternatively, there is nothing sadder than an unloved Leo—they simply shrivel up into depression or bitterness.

Links to Astrology

The Sun symbolizes our essential nature, our individuality, and consciousness. He travels around the zodiac once a year making our birthday our Solar Return—hence "many happy returns of the day."

As a personality, the Sun rules the fire sign of Leo. The Leo archetype could be the person everyone turns to for encouragement and inspiration. They may be over-the-top and bossy, but they are also big-hearted and creative. Leos literally seek out warmth and also seek the sunshine of love and approval.

On a physical level the Sun speaks of health, vitality, and a general sense of wellbeing.

XX

Judgement

The Judgement card depicts a powerful image of rebirth, as a man, woman, and child in the foreground of the picture rise up out of their coffins, arms outstretched and lifted upward in response to the trumpeting of the angel's horn. Other figures are arising from the sea in the background.

JUDGEMENT

Traditional meaning
Renewal, evaluation, new beginnings.

When this card appears in a spread I always draw attention to its symbolism in order to dispel any connotations of harshness or punishment that the word "judgement" might suggest. In fact, this is a positive card, a triumphant announcement of integration and resurrection. It is also the wake-up call, the voice we cannot ignore, which urges us out of the darkness and into the fullness of meaningful life.

Links to Astrology
The Judgement card has overtones of Jupiter, as this is the planet of liberation, new horizons, and rewards. However, the process of symbolic death and rebirth belongs to Pluto, so this card also represents the positive outcome of the Plutonic journey. We are now strengthened and empowered with the benefits of wisdom, knowledge, and experience. In the first instance, Pluto is the agent of annihilation and disintegration, but from the dust we regenerate and salvage that which is really worth having.

The mood of the Judgement card is joyful and celebratory, as the promise of rebirth that we have encountered so many times is now a reality, rather than a hazy concept that we cannot fully grasp. There is also a sense of relief, a feeling of "at last," as the vista of life opens up before us. This is the penultimate card of the Major Arcana, the final stage in the journey before we fully realize that the World is our own. There is a sense of liberation and near completion. The gate is open and now all we have to do is walk through it.

When the Judgement card appears in a spread we know that we are on the right road and that we have already navigated through all kinds of obstacles. The important thing is that we don't stray from the road that has been so difficult to find. This is not the time for hesitation, resistance, or for getting cold feet, but a time for claiming our rewards—our right to happiness and to think well of ourselves.

The main message is that we must be willing to wipe the slate clean and start afresh in light of the lessons we have learned and embrace the decisions that they point to. A brave new world is ours if we can let go of the past, forgive someone else or ourselves, make big changes, and stop putting off until tomorrow what can be done today. Whether this moment of transition comes from our personal development or from a particular experience is irrelevant, as so often our inner and outer worlds are a reflection of each other:

> "*Whatever else is going on around you, there is a push, a call from within, to make some important change. The change can refer to something mundane and immediate, or to an entire shift in the way a person looks at life… In effect, the person has already changed; the old situations, the old self, has already died. It is simply a matter of recognizing it.*" 15

Whatever the context, the Judgement card is ultimately a tribute to the incredible bravery, resilience, and tenacity of the human spirit. Our triumphant moment of rebirth is a celebration of survival.

The Judgement card crossed the Queen of Swords (the widow) for a single mother of 30 at the center of the Celtic Cross. She felt desperately alone, having been abandoned by the father of her child, who didn't want to know after she told him she was pregnant. Her little girl was now six years old and raising her had been a long, tough, and lonely battle.

Most importantly, the Queen of Swords also spoke of her own mother who had been widowed when my client was a small child and who had unwittingly destroyed her daughter's self-esteem by repeatedly telling her that if she had known she was going to be widowed she would never have had children. Affection between them was non-existent.

My client was acutely aware of the repetition, of being a single parent who was unable to show affection. She had had other partners but she admitted that she drove them all away. Her overwhelming need for love and approval was in hopeless conflict with her anger toward men, and the underlying belief that they would leave her anyway. She was an incredibly attractive woman but she believed herself to be plain. Unsurprisingly, the only relationship that had lasted any time at all was with a man who regularly beat her.

As we talked about the Judgement card she said with great fervor that she genuinely wanted to address her problems. She had been resisting therapy for years because "She didn't want to open up a can of worms," which is a classic response of resistance. I replied that it was already open, and that if she chose not to work on her personal development it was putting the lid back on.

I believed that she was already stepping out of the victim role, and that once she committed to counseling she could invoke the message of the Judgement card, start wiping the slate clean, and loosening the stranglehold of repetition that was destroying her own life and could easily destroy her daughter's—the next in line.

the **World**

In the final card of the Major Arcana a maiden, draped in a purple sash and with a wand in each hand, dances on air in celebration. She is encircled and contained by a large laurel wreath, the emblem of success, echoing the triumph of the Six of Wands.

THE WORLD

Traditional meaning
*Completion,
achievement.*

This card rekindles the symbolism of the Wheel of Fortune as here again we see the imagery of wholeness and perpetuity, the world following the rhythmic pattern of its own cycle. We have come full circle and there is a sense of rightness and belonging.

Here is the Fool's goal and final destination, the achievement of full consciousness and integration, in which no function is differentiated. When the World card appears in a reading it points to that moment of arrival, a psychological coming of age in which we find that we have learned the lessons of our inner and outer world and have internalized them.

At a more mundane level the World card announces achievement, a success story, the triumphant realization of a goal, fulfillment, and a happy ending. Some important project or phase of our lives has reached its conclusion and, in this sense, the World card is just as much about beginnings as it is about endings. Success is not about stopping but about moving onward and upward, taking up our rightful place in the world, realizing that the world is our oyster and that we can now forge ahead, living the gift of life to the full.

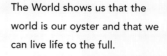

The World shows us that the world is our oyster and that we can live life to the full.

Links to Astrology

In astrology the single most powerful symbol of totality, wholeness, and individuation is the Sun. The glyph for the Sun is simply a circle, the symbol of totality, with a dot in the middle marking the centre of consciousness. No matter what the rest of our horoscope may say, the Sun sign speaks of our essential self, our starting point around which everything else revolves and evolves. In medical astrology the Sun is vital as it rules both the heart and the central structure of the body, the spine.

Interpreting the World

As with the Wheel of Fortune this card is anchored in each corner by images of four signs of the zodiac—a golden-haired man for Aquarius, the eagle for Scorpio, the bull for Taurus and the lion for Leo. These are the four "fixed" signs of the zodiac, the mode that represents solidity, security, and materialization. Each sign represents one of the four elements, which in turn symbolize the four functions of consciousness: Aquarius—air— the intellect and reason, Scorpio—water—feelings and instincts, Taurus—earth—sensation and practicality, Leo—fire— intuition and inspiration.

The World card came up in a spread for a woman in her late forties and was the only Major Arcana card to appear. On the surface her life was content, as she was in a long-term happy marriage, had two wonderful children in their twenties, looked great, and had no financial problems. For a fleeting moment I thought of the hundreds of clients who would willingly trade places with her and, of course, this was the real issue. She knew she had it good and felt that she had no right to be dissatisfied.

She was suffering from the proverbial "empty nest" syndrome, as both children had just left home and a part-time job she had had for years had come to a natural end the previous year. She literally didn't know what to do with herself.

I concentrated on the World card from the angle that one way of life had reached its conclusion and it was time for another to begin.

From my point of view this was a difficult reading as, although she said she found my words encouraging, she didn't have the faintest idea about how to proceed. However, in this instance, astrology came to the rescue, as a look in the Ephemeris told me that she was due for her Jupiter return in about six months' time.

As Jupiter has a 12-year cycle, and thus returns to its natal position every 12 years, I asked her to cast her mind back approximately 12 years ago to the last Jupiter return. What opportunity had presented itself then, or what changes had made life more fulfilling? She had in fact gone to college at this time to learn secretarial skills but had never used them. I suggested that she could now use her free time to study something that she found really interesting. This would put her in touch with like-minded people and would be a way of entering into a whole new World.

The Minor Arcana is made up of 56 cards. This section deals with the first 40, from the Ace through to the Ten for each of the four suits. In the opening sections you will find how each suit compares with the four astrological elements of fire, earth, air, and water. For each card there is a description of its theme and also some anecdotes from my own practice to illustrate the card in its context.

3

THE MINOR ARCANA

the **Minor** Arcana

The Minor Arcana consists of four suits—the Wands, Pentacles, Swords, and Cups—that in ordinary playing cards correlate to the Clubs, Diamonds, Spades, and Hearts. As with ordinary cards, each suit comprises Ace to Ten.

In contrast to ordinary playing cards, the Minor Arcana comprises 56 cards rather than 52, as there are four Court cards for each suit—King, Queen, Knight, and Page—which are dealt with separately in the next chapter.

Some readers will actually separate the Minor and Major Arcanas depending on the kind of spread they want to lay. Others will override a Minor Arcana card if it is laid as the final, outcome card and keep turning the cards until a Major Arcana card appears, which is then taken as "the end of the matter."

However, there are no hard and fast rules as to the relative merits of each Arcana and my own practice is always to use the whole pack. It is important to remember that each card has its own vital role to play in the Fool's journey towards enlightenment. All of life's experiences have a place and the Minor Arcana cards can paint extremely powerful images.

WANDS

In other packs you will find that the Wands are called Staves or Rods. In the Rider-Waite pack the Wands are depicted as long poles, all bearing buds that are blossoming into life. This imagery suggests the presence of a vital life force and the potential for growth. The Wands are used in a variety of ways depending on the

Trials and tribulations

The word "minor" immediately suggests that these cards are of lesser importance and, on the whole, I have found that they do tend to speak of life's trials and tribulations rather than signalling major life changes or turning points.

The Wands vary in their symbolic meaning but often signify new life or growth.

situation symbolized. They may be brandished as weapons in battle, held as protection, or raised aloft in triumph.

PENTACLES

The Pentacles are illustrated as coins, each one carrying the emblem of the five-pointed star. As a symbol the Pentacle is steeped in magic and is associated with both paganism and Christian mysticism. It can be drawn in one continuous line, symbolizing protection. In the Tarot the Pentacles relate mostly to financial or practical matters and they illustrate how we make, receive, spend, save, or use our money and resources. They illustrate the spectrum of poverty through to wealth.

The Pentacles are usually associated with practical matters such as money.

The Swords can symbolize attack, defense, and emotional problems.

SWORDS

As a symbol the sword is invested with enormous power. It appears in countless stories and myths, such as Arthur's Excalibur and the Sword of Damocles. It is the ultimate phallic symbol of strength, virility, and bravery. The Swords, like the Wands, can be used either for attack or defense. Swords can cut and wound so they symbolize emotional hurt and pain as much as strife. They can also symbolize the problems created by inaction through lack of courage or purpose.

CUPS

The element of water symbolizes the emotions, and as water can only take the shape of the vessel into which it is poured, the Cups carry all that is to do with feeling. They illustrate the whole range of happiness, from falling in love to raising our cups in joy and celebration. They also illustrate the emotional pain of life's trials, such as loss, love gone wrong, or disappointments. Unhappiness is sometimes shown by the Cups going unnoticed or being overturned, with the water soaking away into the ground.

LINKS TO ASTROLOGY

We have seen how the Major Arcana cards equate to the symbolism of the slower moving planets, such as Jupiter for the Wheel of Fortune, Uranus for the Tower, and Pluto for Death or the Devil. The Minor Arcana cards work in the same way, but we can also include the swifter moving bodies—the Moon, Mercury, Venus, and Mars—as you will see in the introduction to each section. You will find a description of each element and its qualities in the introduction to each section.

The Cups represent the whole range of emotions, from happiness to pain.

Links to Astrology
As well as echoing planetary symbolism, the four suits correspond to the four elements in the following order:

Wands
Fire — Aries, Leo, Sagittarius.

Pentacles
Earth — Taurus, Virgo, Capricorn.

Swords
Air — Gemini, Libra, Aquarius.

Cups
Water — Cancer, Scorpio, Pisces.

WANDS

Sometimes called Rods or Staves, the Wands symbolize our creative and artistic ability. They also stand for our energy, our drive, and how we deal with situations that stimulate our personal development. The potential for growth is symbolized by the buds on the wands preparing to burst into leaf.

♂ ♃

Links to Astrology
The wands match the symbolism of:

Mars *The planet of action and war.*

Jupiter *The planet of expansion, knowledge, and good fortune.*

The Wands represent the element of fire and also rule your creative energy, artistic ability, and intuitive powers.

IN ASTROLOGICAL TERMS
The Wands correspond to fire, the element that rules our energy, creativity, and intuition. The main qualities and characteristics symbolized by fire can be found in the following keywords and phrases:

Positive Warm, friendly, affectionate, demonstrative, spontaneous, intuitive, generous, bold, loyal, courageous, inspired, visionary, honest, sense of justice and fair play, enthusiastic, quick, lively, dynamic, vivacious, optimistic, adventurous, confident, assertive, independent, self-starting, enterprising.

Negative Rash, reckless, words spoken in the heat of the moment, explosive, quick, fiery temper, inflammatory, feverish, over-impulsive, careless, things started but not finished, burnout, selfish, lack of tact or diplomacy, proud, intolerant, aggressive, abrasive, strong tendency to exaggerate and dramatize.

the Ace of Wands

ACE OF WANDS

Quite simply, Aces are the number one card of each suit and so they symbolize beginnings—and the Ace of Wands represents opportunity, especially regarding a new project. Often, this is something which is creative, requiring our enthusiasm and a degree of originality.

If there are no obvious artistic, creative, or spiritual correlations, the Ace of Wands can mean a new job that will open new doors, the chance to learn new skills to help you climb the professional ladder, or sometimes the opportunity to travel.

As with all the Aces, the single wand is offered by a hand emerging from a cloud, so there is a sense of providence or divine intervention, a helping hand. It is up to us to grasp the wand, to broaden our horizons, and to bring our own initiative into play. The Ace of Wands reminds us that the positive fiery qualities, such as confidence and enthusiasm, are our strongest assets at the beginning of any new project or adventure.

The Ace of Wands often points to the theme of vocation, the things that we really want to do and that inspire us. For example, this Ace was a pivotal card for a young man who was about to write a book. Part of his quandary was that he needed to create more time and was gearing up to leave full-time employment and take a part-time job. All he needed was encouragement and reassurance that the time was ripe for taking the plunge.

This card also appeared for an actress who was about to leave a well-known soap opera and branch out into more serious drama. This move was not without risk, as her name and face would disappear from daily television and, in a sense, she would be starting her career all over again. But she was excited at the offers that were starting to come in, which would set her on a whole new path.

In both of these examples, money was not the prime motivation. In fact, there was the likelihood of *less* money at the beginning of the venture. However, both individuals were prepared to accept this situation because of the need to satisfy the creative urge, to do what they felt they were supposed to be doing.

the **2** of **Wands**

II

A well-dressed man stands on the battlements and surveys the land before him. He holds one Wand in his left hand and a small globe of the world in his right. The other Wand stands upright behind him.

Whereas the Aces tend to point to a single course of action, the Twos are often about choices, dilemmas, or union. Another factor has come into play.

There is a certain restlessness, maybe the first stirrings of discontent, as you become aware of new horizons. There is a sense of having reached a crossroads and now the direction to take needs to be pondered and decided. The pros and cons of a situation need to be weighed up.

In my own readings this card has frequently shown for someone who is deciding where to be in a geographical sense. The Two of Wands indicates a growing awareness that there is more to the world than your own back yard. It brings a yearning, or a wondering, and there is a choice to be made. Emigrating can be a serious consideration but, because the world is your oyster, the choices may be overwhelming.

Whatever the particular situation, the message is that there is the choice between staying put or moving on, either literally or within a situation.

the **3** of **Wands**

III

In the Two of Wands the man holds the globe in his hand. In the Three of Wands the figure has his back to us and stares out toward the distant horizon.

In many ways, the message is the same as for the Two of Wands—there's a big world out there and there are decisions to be made about what to do, where to go, and how to get there. This figure, however, has now descended from the battlements and looks out from the top of a mountain. There is a sense that we are on our way.

There is still an element of thought and deliberation, as this card signals the planning stage of an idea or venture. The Three of Pentacles also carries this theme, but more at a financial or practical level. The Three of Wands relates more to seeking good fortune at a personal, spiritual level. This card can often mean that you are looking for a way forward, knowing that the answers are out there but not yet knowing how to find them. There is a sense of gearing up for action before taking the plunge. I have also seen this card in the context of homesickness or wistfulness—your heart is elsewhere, with someone in a distant place, but for the time being you are kept at a distance.

the **4** of **Wands**

The four Wands create a doorway into a castle, portraying security and prosperity. The tops of the wands are garlanded and the two main figures, a happy couple, hold aloft their own flowers in greeting.

IV

The number four is often associated with stability and that which is grounded and fixed, such as the four corners of a house or the four points of the compass, the flip side of the coin being immobility or that which is stuck. The Four of Wands, however, shows the positive side of this concept, often symbolizing safety and prosperity.

It is a helpful device for the Tarot reader to give each card a personal name, and I'm probably not the first reader to call the Four of Wands the "Happy Homecoming" card. It often shows when you are preparing for a reunion of some kind, perhaps with a partner, or with members of your family. It can also symbolize a new home, or happiness within the home, marriage or moving in with a partner. Or it may just signal holidays and time for relaxation.

The Four of Wands was the outcome card in a reading for a young woman, preceded by the Lovers and the Six of Wands, which speaks of triumph. She was busy with plans for her wedding later that summer, which was set to be the event of the year, involving many family members on both sides. The theme of reunion was very strong, as this would be the first time in years that all of her family would be together at the same time. She also was planning the honeymoon and the decorating and furnishing of a new home. This reading was an example of someone with no particular issues or problems. She said she was just interested to see if the coming events would show—and she was delighted that they did.

The Four of Wands is often called the "Happy Homecoming" card, showing when there is some sort of reunion taking place.

the 5 of Wands

V

Five young men are locked in battle, each one brandishing a Wand as a weapon.

This card is sometimes said to depict playful fighting but, in my own experience, there is nothing particularly playful about the Five of Wands. On the contrary, it tends to show when someone is involved in, or surrounded by ongoing arguments, office politics, other people's squabbling, or backbiting of some kind. This card is disruptive and quarrelsome, pointing to discord, small-mindedness, or petty troublemaking.

Obviously, a lot depends on context, but you will hear stories that range from upsetting to plain tiresome. However, whether the conflict is with friends, family, or colleagues, or whether it is a clash with someone who has power over you, the Five of Wands generally points to matters which are not destructive in a major way. The problems or upset may be difficult or painful to deal with at the time, but they tend to blow over without serious harm being done. Relationships that are impaired as a result of this kind of conflict are those that you can do without.

The Five of Wands usually signifies that a client needs to put up some firm boundaries, to put some distance between him- or herself and a source of trouble, and most definitely not to fight other people's battles for them.

This was the advice I gave to a girl in her early twenties who was working her first summer season in Greece as part of a small team, and it was not the idyll she had dreamed about. There were constant bickerings, frayed tempers, and "ganging up" behaviour—an almost inevitable result of an inexperienced and badly managed team of young people, some away from home and working for the first time. Throw in a searing temperature of around 100°F (38°C) and you have the ultimate boiling pot. My client did manage to stand back from the crowd, made some new friends elsewhere, and left at the end of the season— needless to say, without the addresses or telephone numbers of her team-mates.

the **6** of **Wands**

*This card shows a young man riding down the street in triumph,
holding one of the Wands, which is adorned with a laurel wreath.
The other Wands are held aloft by the crowd lining the street,
cheering him forward.*

VI

The Six of Wands is the success card. It points to achievement, which brings praise and recognition. In my own readings, this card has shown for things such as weddings, passing exams or a driving test, or the successful outcome of a tough situation. Again, the context is all-important, but generally the rewards are deserved and any ongoing matter is destined for glory.

This card came up for a young woman who was setting up her own business. She was getting increasingly nervous because she was pouring every penny she had into this project and was having difficulty securing some crucial documents. She was beginning to wonder if she should cut her losses and pull out. The reading reflected these problems, the central card being the Five of Wands, which she identified as doing battle with authorities. Happily, the outcome card was the Six of Wands, which suggested that she would win through in the end. The business continues to thrive.

the **7** of **Wands**

*One man uses one of the Wands to ward off the other six, which are
being brandished by unseen assailants.*

VII

The Seven of Wands is the card of self-defense. However, I have never seen it in the context of someone needing to defend him- or herself from physical violence, although this possibility should not be ruled out if it appears alongside Swords or the heavier Major Arcana cards.

This card often points to the need to defend your territory and space, such as protecting yourself from someone who is bad for you or who bullies you. It reminds you of the importance of standing up for yourself. In this respect it is a card of valor and bravery and it is important to make a firm stand. It also can indicate taking up the role of protector for a loved one. Again, as with the Five of Wands, I advise not to fight other people's battles for them, unless it is a case of defending someone who is unable to stand up for him- or herself.

This was the case with a woman who was having problems with her neighbors. Her son had started playing with the boy from this family, who she felt was a bad influence because he was spoilt and prone to bullying. The appearance of the Seven of Wands justified her defensive instincts.

the 8 of Wands

VIII

Apart from the Ace, in which the Wand is offered by a hand from the clouds, the Eight of Wands is the only card in the suit that does not depict people. Instead, the eight Wands slant downward across the card, against a simple background of a river running through fields. They can be seen as flying through the air and about to land.

This is the card of movement and progress, and often it is a case of events conspiring to move things on, rather than human effort. It usually signifies that a period of waiting is coming to an end, the time is right for change, and expected or desired events will start to unfold. There is often an attendant feeling of freedom, either in the physical sense or in the sense of being liberated from emotional restraints that have been holding us back or causing us problems or pain. It signals the end of delays and the removal of obstacles, so this is a card of success and satisfaction.

In my own readings I have seen this card in the context of waiting for exam results, job applications, or news that will make a positive difference. Also, this card often points to travel, especially going abroad, so holidays, a break, or a stress-free period are all possibilities.

the 9 of Wands

IX

The card shows a man entrenched in a battle scene, his head is bandaged, and he clutches one of the Wands while the other eight are impaled in the ground behind him as if to create a barricade.

As we near the end of the suit there is extreme difficulty or stress to contend with. This is the "battle weary" card, and it invariably shows when someone is in the thick of some kind of ordeal or endurance test. The figure in the card is bloodied but not bowed, so the main message is that even if you are feeling wounded or reaching the end of your tether, you are still standing and prepared to battle on, even if it takes your last ounce of strength.

I have seen this card for relationships that have gone horribly wrong, for people who are going through an especially difficult divorce process, or for people who are under a great deal of stress and trying to hang on to a job. But whatever the context, the important thing to remember is that the battle is not over. The watchfulness of the wounded and embattled figure suggests the need for continued vigilance and self-protection.

the **10** of **Wands**

X

Unlike the Nine of Wands, the figure in the Ten of Wands is not wounded, but he is completely bowed down with his burden of all ten Wands. We cannot see his face, and he in turn can hardly see where he is going as he is so encumbered. All he can do is put one foot in front of the other as he feels his way forward.

Not surprisingly, this card often shows when work pressures, a particular situation, or responsibility has become too much to bear. When this card comes up, I always try to find out what can be done to ease the situation. When we are seriously stressed, we sometimes forget to look up and look around, and end up missing out on help that we might otherwise get. Or it may be that we are deliberately not looking, believing that others should notice our plight and rescue us without having to be told. Either way, the experience of being weighed down may be unavoidable for the time being, but there is no harm in trying to find a way to share the load or to enlist moral support, and any kind of martyrdom is not the answer.

The Nine of Wands

described the recent past in a Celtic Cross spread for a client who was newly married with a six-month-old baby. I suggested that she had recently been at breaking point, which she confirmed. However, her story clearly indicated that this card described her husband's life even more than her own. He had just asked to be demoted because he never saw his wife and child and the strain on his marriage had been so great that he could foresee divorce. He had opted for less money in order to create more time for his family.

The Ten of Wands

came up as the central card for a woman in her fifties. In conjunction with the Emperor, the card of patriarchal power and authority, I felt that she was in a situation of intimidation. The story that emerged confirmed the worst, that she was so oppressed by her husband that she literally could see no way forward. He sabotaged all her efforts to communicate with him—if she tried to talk to him, he would turn away; if she wrote him a letter, he would throw it in the bin. Anger was always his initial response, coupled with a refusal to help in the house or to show any interest in her work. She felt trapped, belittled, and exhausted at every level.

In a situation like this it is hard to know where to start. However, drawing attention to the card validated her experience, and I asked her to visualize laying down this load, and also to consider what she could see by looking up and out of the situation.

PENTACLES

The Pentacles—sometimes called Coins or Discs—are invariably about money and our material world. However, they also sometimes carry a message connected with self-worth and the value we attach to things, to others, to our work, and so on.

Links to Astrology
Pentacles match the symbolism of:

Venus *The planet of love and pleasure, which also rules money*

Saturn *The planet of work, order, and all practical issues.*

The Pentacles correlate to the element of earth, describing practical situations, or people who are largely close to nature, reliable, steady, and secure.

IN ASTROLOGICAL TERMS
Pentacles correspond to earth, the element that rules the sensations, nature, and all things practical and tangible. The main qualities and characteristics symbolized by earth can be found in the following list of keywords and phrases:

Positive Practical, pragmatic, capable, reliable, industrious, careful, conscientious, sensual, tactile, comforting, unflappable, unshockable, placid, a rock, steady, secure, stoic, patient, kind-hearted, grounded, providers, earthy sense of humor, courteous, sense of purpose, goal-orientated, persevering.

Negative Stuck, heavy-going, sluggish, ponderous, pedantic, stick-in-the mud, over-cautious, over-serious, avaricious, overly concerned with money and materialism, stubborn, resistant to change, unimaginative, thick-skinned, pessimistic, non risk-taking, black-and-white approach to everything.

the Ace of Pentacles

Aces are beginnings, so the Ace of Pentacles can represent a fresh start with money. This can materialize in a variety of ways, such as a pay rise, extra cash coming in from another quarter, or a lump sum of money in the shape of a loan, a gift, or even a bequest. Or it can indicate a new job or business opportunity which can lead to prosperity. It can also sometimes represent a gift of great value, such as jewellery or gold.

FINANCIAL SETBACKS

If the Ace appears alongside troublesome cards, then look out for a disappointment or setback regarding money matters. In a difficult reading for a young woman who was expecting her first child, the Ace was the center card of the Celtic Cross spread and it was crossed by the Page of Swords.

This Page is unreliable at best, deceitful at worst, and in this case it proved to be her partner, who had rather a checkered history in the course of their long-term relationship. They were not married but he was planning to move in with her now that she was expecting a baby, and when she first fell pregnant he had immediately put aside a large sum of money for the baby. However, in the following months this money had been gradually spent on various other things and, at the time of the reading, it had nearly all disappeared. So, in this case, the Ace of Pentacles was indeed a sum of money for a specific purpose, but money which was destined never to reach her.

ACE OF PENTACLES

The Ace of Pentacles appeared as the immediate future card in a reading for a woman in her forties, with no obvious job prospects or opportunities looming. As I talked about the card and what it meant, she just shook her head and said that she couldn't imagine more money coming in so quickly, but she sincerely hoped I was right. She told me six weeks later that her sister had won some money on the lottery and had sent her a cheque.

However, I have generally found that the Ace of Pentacles relates to work matters or that it points to money for a specific purpose or reason. For example, this card came up as a past card for a woman who confirmed that she had just received $4,500 from her parents so that she could buy a car.

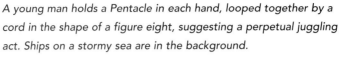

the **2** of **Pentacles**

A young man holds a Pentacle in each hand, looped together by a cord in the shape of a figure eight, suggesting a perpetual juggling act. Ships on a stormy sea are in the background.

This card speaks clearly for itself. It frequently shows when money is tight and finances have to be juggled in order to make ends meet, or it's a case of robbing Peter to pay Paul, or even doing two jobs. This card often indicates change around money matters but this is not always easy, obvious, or straightforward. The skill of the juggler indicates that it is important to keep things moving and at exactly the right pace. Timing is everything. Also the ships being tossed on a stormy sea in the background can mean that a situation, not necessarily financial, may be more precarious than is at first realized. You are so busy keeping different balls in the air that you don't notice the slow descent into chaos. Alternatively, you may know that a situation is potentially disastrous, but you simply turn your back on it and ignore it, either because there is currently no other option or because you don't want to confront reality.

If there are no obvious financial correlations with this card, it can point to someone expending all of their energy on holding it together. Any situation that is tricky, or that requires some kind of balancing act, needs to be addressed. The Two of Pentacles reminds you that positive, earthy qualities, such as being pragmatic, practical, and resourceful, will help you to resolve a dilemma so that you can stop wasting energy on merely maintaining a negative status quo.

The Two of Pentacles frequently shows the need to juggle personal finances.

II

the **3** of **Pentacles**

Three figures stand in front of a double archway—a well-dressed couple consulting with a professional craftsman.

III

In the suit of Wands the Three carries the message of gearing up for action, and this theme is repeated with the Three of Pentacles, but this time with regard to money matters or specific projects as opposed to personal or spiritual fulfillment. This card indicates that there are negotiations afoot regarding making money, such as starting a business or taking up a promotion. It can also relate to spending money already accrued, such as buying property or making investments.

Invariably this card indicates the need or presence of a third party whose expertise is required. This could be a bank manager, a managing director, a solicitor, or an architect.

When this card represents a new venture or project, I usually ask if there is some kind of professional help or guidance on hand and, if not, recommend that it be sought. Attention to detail at this stage is crucial, as the final results will only be as good as the preparatory work. This is a card of laying foundations, devoting time to research, and learning the art of skillful negotiation.

the **4** of **Pentacles**

A man sits with his four Pentacles safely attached to him—one in his hands, one on the top of his head, and the other two under his feet.

IV

At best, this is a card of caution—of carefully guarding your resources and holding on firmly to what you have earned or accumulated.

However, the figure is a well-dressed man of the city and wears a crown, so how far is this caution justified? At worst this is a card of meanness, being well-off but unwilling to share. However, it can also indicate fear—clinging to material security in the belief that this is all that matters and that it could be taken away.

There may be a lot of underlying anxiety when this card appears. Someone could be so anxious about a situation, financial or otherwise, that he or she has simply seized up. There is a refusal or inability to move as all his or her energy is fed into holding on and preserving the status quo. This kind of blockage works two ways—nothing may be going out, but there is no room for anything to come in, either. As long as you are in this paralysis, nothing can change. Whatever the predicament there is a strong need to let go, lighten up, and create a movement in energy or a cash flow.

the **5** of **Pentacles**

V

Showing two paupers—one on crutches, out in the snow—the Five of Pentacles is a card of hardship. The five Pentacles are framed in a stained glass window, indicating a church, but the two homeless figures seem to have no way of entering into the world behind this window, or may not even be aware of the window at all.

This is clearly a card of poverty in the financial sense and it can show when someone is out of work, or unable to work through illness or disability, or just struggling to make ends meet. But it can also be a card of spiritual poverty, so this card can appear when someone feels that life has become meaningless. There is also a sense of being out in the cold metaphorically, so even if help has been sought it may have been denied. Or it may be that someone is desperately lonely, shut out from the world of someone whom they would dearly love to be with. Whatever the particular situation, it is clear that help is needed, and measures need to be taken to start putting matters to rights, either financially or emotionally.

the **6** of **Pentacles**

VI

The Six of Pentacles shows an affluent man holding a set of scales in one hand, while his other drops coins into the upturned palms of one of two beggars kneeling at his feet.

This is primarily a card of repayment—either money owing to you is about to be repaid, or money that you owe to others needs to be settled up. Either way, it's a case of balancing the books.

There is also a theme of charity in this card, as the figure handing out the money is clearly well-off and in a position to share his good fortune. This speaks of someone with a kind and generous nature. Depending on the context of the reading, you will either receive help, financial or otherwise, from such a person, or you may be the one who is able to offer help to those in genuine need.

The presence of the scales is always a symbol of fairness and balance, so it is important to see where this theme comes into play. There may be a need to give something back, to show appreciation of support or favors. If there is no obvious benefactor in the picture, this card can also mean the need to borrow or arrange a loan.

the **7** of **Pentacles**

A young man rests on his hoe and contemplates the seven Pentacles heaped up before him.

VII

This is a card of assessment and deliberation, a time for reflecting on how far you have come within a situation or with a project. It often indicates achievement, as progress is already substantial, but there is still more to be done and a lot further to go. This is but a pause in your labors.

When this card appears it often speaks of a crossroads of some kind. Choices may have to be made, either to continue along the same road or to take up something new. You have yet to see if your further efforts will be fruitful or worthwhile.

Usually the main message is to continue, and that to pause for too long would be a mistake. It is time to capitalize on the work that is already done. I have seen this card appear in the context of working at a relationship, but more often than not it tends to relate to our projects and ambitions, often those that have a long time span.

The Seven of Pentacles showed the state of mind of one young man when he was halfway through a degree course. The temptation to drop out and give up was very strong—so my first step was to assure him that this feeling was one that many students experience when the pressure is on and passing exams seems like an unreachable goal. Although the amount of work still to be done appeared overwhelming, the important thing was to look at what he had already achieved, and buoy up his flagging energies by reminding himself that it would be a pity to give up now when he had come this far.

When this card appears, it often shows a situation that requires faith and perseverance, from which we will reap many rewards if we are able to see it through to its conclusion.

the 8 of Pentacles

VIII

A young man sits astride his work bench, chiseling the design on one of his Pentacles. Six are already finished and stacked up in front of him, while one remains on the floor waiting to be done.

This card nearly always indicates a period of hard work, but not necessarily a slog. It is the card of the craftsperson, so it's a time for perfecting skills that you already have or for learning new ones that will bring you greater earning power.

Work opportunities and new projects are often indicated by this card, and there's also a sense of taking pride in a job well done for its own sake.

The Eight of Pentacles appeared as the central card in the Celtic Cross in a reading for a young woman, crossed by the Eight of Wands, which stands for movement and progress. She had recently applied for a job for which she had been turned down. However, her real wish was to travel—so here was another "take" on the Eight of Pentacles being crossed by the Eight of Wands. She wanted to be on the move but was being held back by thinking she needed to get a job.

the 9 of Pentacles

IX

The Nine depicts a beautifully dressed and obviously wealthy woman, at home in lovely and fertile surroundings. The feel of the card is one of abundance, serenity, and safety.

As we reach the end of the suit of Pentacles, we find prosperity and, as with the Cups, the Nine and the Ten of the suit are the best.

The woman's only companion is the bird perched on her wrist. This is a bird of prey, presumably a falcon, as it perches on her gloved hand. Falconry is a sport of the rich, with connotations of aristocracy and the leisured class of society, so here is real wealth, or even "old money," or the clear message that money is simply not a problem for her.

There is also a sense of solitude with this card, but this is very different from loneliness. When this card appears I have found that it nearly always points to a time of being alone in the physical sense, but that there is provision being made in some kind of way.

When this card appears a partner may be temporarily absent, or it may be that someone is able to enjoy being single in a positive way, relishing the advantages and benefits of autonomy. Often this is someone who has built their own security

the 10 of Pentacles

Three generations adorn the Ten of Pentacles—a grandfather, a couple, their child, and two dogs, clearly family pets, again in rich and colorful surroundings.

The Ten of Pentacles represents the ultimate prosperity and security, often as a result of wealth or generosity within the family unit. It can also symbolize money or property that is the result of many years of hard work.

When this card appears in a reading, it can mean that there is financial assistance coming from the family. There may also be emotional support, but either way there is a relative who has both the desire and the means to help out where help is needed. It can also indicate an inheritance or amicable distribution of money or goods within the family.

Money may also come from other sources, but especially from a group or organization that is well established and already profitable. Whatever the particular context, this card means that finances will improve in some way. If this is through work, then there's the possibility of a new job, a great business opportunity, or a brilliant promotion.

and can happily wait for the right person to share it with.

This card is also a reminder that inner peace and contentment ultimately come from ourselves, not another person. You may need a space in your life in which to learn how to be in harmony with your surroundings before you try to fill your world with other people.

The Nine of Pentacles came up for a woman whose husband was about to go away to work at sea. He would be away for several months, but they already had plenty of money, and his earning potential was huge. Although she knew she would have to cope with their young family alone for a while, she had no qualms about this, being a down-to-earth and materialistic Taurean. She openly admitted that money was extremely important to her and that both she and her husband saw this time as a real opportunity—the chance to build even more financial security for the future.

SWORDS

Swords are weapons, so we use them either for attack or for defense, for fight or flight. Either way, we are pulled into conflict. The Swords speak of how we deal with strife and battle in our lives, how we react, and how we deal with our adversaries or with our inner struggles.

Links to Astrology
Swords match the symbolism of:

Mercury The planet of the mind and how we communicate.

Mars The planet of action and strife, who in mythology is the god of war.

The Swords represent the element of air. They are also weapons and can signify a variety of difficult emotions.

Swords can wound, either ourselves or another, so these cards speak of pain, anguish, anger, and a host of uncomfortable emotions. In this respect the Swords are the most difficult of the suits, as none of the cards, with the exception of the Ace, are easy or joyful.

IN ASTROLOGICAL TERMS
The Swords correspond to air, the element that rules the intellect and the abstract. The main qualities and characteristics symbolized by air can be found in the following lists of keywords and phrases:

Positive Quick, intelligent, intellectual, analytical, inventive, original, articulate, communicative, brilliant conversationalists, versatile, easy-going, a light touch, breath of fresh air, curious, interested, aware, objective, rational, systematic, scientific, ethical.

Negative Didactic, argumentative, lacking in empathy, overly matter-of-fact, black-and-white, dismissive, unbalanced, fanatical, eccentric, misfits, cynical, mean, out of touch with reality, over-principled, inflexible, blinkered, indecisive, apathetic.

the **Ace** of **Swords**

ACE OF SWORDS

Aces are beginnings and, as with the three other suits, the Aces speak of opportunity and fresh starts. This is also the case with the Ace of Swords, but there is the sense that a challenge is being offered and that it is up to you to seize the Sword and wield it with all your strength and determination. This card often shows for a new venture or enterprise, usually one that is just beginning but sometimes one that may still be in an embryonic stage. This Sword is crowned, so the pursuit of a challenge or realizing an ambition is clearly destined for success.

This card can also represent the sword of truth and justice, so it can show when you are taking up a cause or fighting on someone else's behalf. But whatever the context, this card indicates the need for courage, resourcefulness, or single-mindedness. You may need to exert the full force of your personality in order to achieve your goal.

The Ace of Swords indicated the immediate future for a young woman who was just about to start her own business on the Internet. She realized that it would take a lot of guts and that she would be on her own, at least at the outset. The business would fail or succeed on the strength of her own efforts, but I pointed out the crown on the Sword and encouraged her to have faith, both in the project and in the power of her initiative. Her ideas were brilliant, and it seemed to me that she was already one step ahead of any possible competition.

Note also how the symbolism of the card perfectly fits the project. She was not especially motivated by a sense of adventure, or a desire to satisfy the creative urge (Wands), or even the desire to make a lot of money (Pentacles), but with realizing an idea which was still just a concept. Also, in astrological symbolism, computers and technology relate to the element of air, so a new business on the Internet is accurately symbolized by this Ace.

the **2** of **Swords**

II

A woman sits blindfolded with her back to the sea, balancing two very long swords in her hands, which are folded across her chest.

This card tends to show when you are in some kind of mental paralysis, unable to make a decision or to act assertively. You ignore what is going on around you in a futile attempt to preserve the status quo.

The Two of Swords is the proverbial ostrich burying its head in the sand—if you ignore troubles they might go away, or you may be able to convince yourself that they aren't there at all. But the twos often imply choices, and when this card shows, you need to overcome your fear of tackling something unpleasant.

The Two of Swords came up in a spread for a woman in her late twenties. It was the card indicating the recent past and it was preceded by the Lovers. This combination suggested indecision in her love life. This she confirmed, and she added that she had wanted to finish her relationship for some time. She admitted to difficulty with endings of any kind, but could see how her life would remain stuck until she became the agent of change and was active rather than passive.

the **3** of **Swords**

III

This card is one of the more dramatic images in the Tarot, as it shows three Swords piercing a heart against a background of rain and cloud.

At best this is an attack of the blues, a bitter disappointment, or a setback, but at worst it is heartbreak, pain, and suffering caused by someone or something that has wounded you deeply. Either way, this is a dismal picture, and when this card appears it is often a case of having to wait for the sun to come out again.

In the meantime you face a period of sorrow, disillusionment, or even rage against an individual or the world. How quickly you recover depends on how soon you are able to let go and move on, rather than giving in to bitterness or cynicism.

This scenario came up for a woman in her mid-forties whose husband had left her for another woman. She was a Scorpio and you cannot beat this sign for *"Heaven has no rage like love to hatred turned/Nor hell a fury like a woman scorned."*[16] The split had happened a year ago, but she was still hellbent on revenge and openly stated, "I don't want him to be happy." From all accounts, however, it seemed that he *was* happy, in spite of all her efforts to sabotage his new relationship. I had to point out that the only person who was suffering was herself.

the **4** of **Swords**

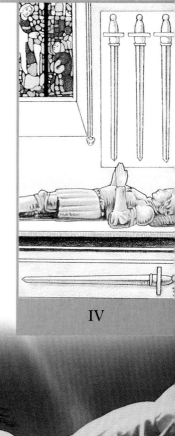

A man lies on his tomb with three swords suspended on the wall behind him and one by his side.

At first sight this looks like a death card, but note that the man holds his hands together, pointing toward the ceiling, as if in prayer. However, this is the only sign of life or movement in a card that is otherwise totally still.

The Four of Swords often shows for illness, especially at a time of recovery, and I usually refer to it as "the convalescence card." I have generally found this card to speak of quite major illness—serious conditions or operations that put us out of action. If the Four of Swords appears with other difficult cards, an illness may even have been life-threatening. If it appears as a future card, I always urge the person to take care of his or her health and to look after him- or herself as much as possible.

In a spread for a young woman this card appeared as a past card along with the Hermit, a card of retreat and time out, so this combination suggested that she really had been laid low. She confirmed that she had just come out of hospital after a burst appendix had resulted in peritonitis, a potentially life-threatening condition. In fact, she had thought she was going to die and the experience had been traumatic at both a physical and emotional level. Happily, the card for her current situation was the Star, a card of healing and renewal, and her outcome card was the Sun, pointing to good health,

energy, and success. I had no hesitation in predicting a total recovery and that she might find that she had more vitality and lust for life than ever.

As well as physical recuperation, the Four of Swords can also indicate a time of emotional healing after trauma or a painful experience of some kind.

The Four of Swords is often "the convalescence card," showing recovery and healing after a period of illness or trauma.

IV

the 5 of Swords

A man stands victorious holding three of the Swords while the other two lie on the ground, seemingly discarded by the two beaten men who are retreating from the conflict.

This is the card of defeat and it can show when you are up against an adversary who is just too strong for you, or someone who cannot give you what you want. Coming to this realization is a painful process and, depending on the position of the card, there has already been a battle, one is raging, or one is about to happen.

In my own experience this card indicates a serious falling out rather than just a petty squabble. This may be due to a clash of personalities or a battle of wills. The main message of this card is to walk away from a destructive situation, as you are almost certainly fighting a losing battle. However, if someone is really determined to repair the damage and heal a rift, or if other cards indicate reconciliation, I usually suggest a cooling-off period first. Not much can be achieved when tempers are running high. If you recognize yourself in the victor, however, you need to question what you have won or hope to win. It may turn out to be a hollow victory and the taste of "success" can very quickly turn sour.

The Five of Swords appeared in a reading for a man in his late forties who was in his second marriage. The honeymoon period had worn off and there had been a bitter falling out over money problems and accusations of neglect on both sides, followed by a period of emotional and physical estrangement. This picture was aptly illustrated by the sequence of the Five of Pentacles (financial and/or emotional bleakness), the Tower (splits and trauma), and the Four of Cups (dis-spiritedness and despondency.)

He had ended up walking out, but admitted that he had acted in anger, while secretly believing that she would have him back at the drop of a hat. When she didn't he realized that his moment of "victory" had been short-lived, not to say self-defeating. His question now was would she come back? We talked about the need to put an end to fighting and blaming, or any kind of game-playing, and with the Two of Cups as the outcome card I was able to assure him that a reunion was still possible and desired on both sides.

the **6** of **Swords**

Two hunched figures of a woman and child are being ferried across a
river. All six Swords are being carried with them, standing upright
before them in the boat.

A journey, literal or metaphorical, is indicated by the Six of Swords and I often call this "the card of passage."

The sense of grieving in this card means that a journey may have to be made for sad reasons, and on a couple of occasions I have seen this card show for someone who has had to travel to a funeral. There is a parallel here with the mythology of the ferryman taking his passengers across the river Styx.

More usually, though, the journey is necessary, the alternative being to stay in a situation that is no longer helpful, healthy, or viable. The sadness of separation will soon be healed when you find yourself in a better space. In this sense this card is often a case of head over heart, and it is ultimately a card of self-development and progress. For example, this card appeared for a woman who was facing a long period of separation from her partner, who was going to work away from home. She knew she had to focus on the benefits of this decision, despite the pain it caused her.

VI

the **7** of **Swords**

A man flees from a camp, holding five of the Swords in his arms and
leaving the other two impaled in the ground behind him. He may be
a thief, making his getaway with all that he can carry.

A t first glance this card is very similar to the Five of Swords. However, the Seven depicts a different kind of defeat, as this is a card of flight not fight, escaping from a situation rather than staying and battling it out.

This card conjures up stealth and the use of cunning in order to extricate yourself from a difficult situation. This is not necessarily a bad thing and some situations are best handled by retreat.

However, I have often found that this card shows when someone is feeling guilty about the way that he or she has handled something, maybe because he or she feels that someone has been let down. There is a lack of assertiveness, stealing away rather than confronting the issue. If the card is a significator for someone else, it can mean that this person is feeling guilty about you, or is fearful of your reaction to something. Or this person may be sidestepping his or her responsibilities or avoiding you for some reason. Some kind of confrontation can be useful, and I usually discuss how matters can be brought into the open.

VII

the **8** of **Swords**

VIII

A woman stands amongst the eight Swords, all impaled in the ground. She is blindfolded, roped, and tied so that her arms are pinioned behind her. Note, however, that her legs are free to move.

This card means that you feel backed into a corner, trapped, or imprisoned by someone or by your circumstances. Yet, in spite of feeling hemmed in, you can still walk away if only you realize that you can. This card is about power—have you given your power to someone else and allowed him or her to call all the shots? To what extent are you underestimating or disregarding your power and authority?

I usually discuss the notion of choice when this card appears as, when we feel trapped by a situation, a relationship, or even an obsession—and I have seen examples of all three scenarios—we often lose sight of the fact that we still have options. With the Eight of Swords you will often hear the words, "I can't," to which the answer is always, "Why not?"

Awakening the idea that you may be in a certain state of your own making leads you to the realization that you can also remove yourself from this state. Reaching this point of painful awareness is, however, difficult, and the misery and frustration of this card should not be underestimated.

the **9** of **Swords**

IX

A figure sits upright in bed, head in hands, the picture of despair. The nine Swords are stacked horizontally on the wall behind this figure, but they do not impale the body as they do in the Ten of this suit.

I call this "the anxiety card," and it is often an anxiety or angst which is spiraling out of control. When this card appears it can mean that you are tormenting yourself with your own worst fears, but these fears may not be as bad as you imagine. The real problem is more likely to be that you have become isolated, feeling that you are alone with a problem and convinced that there is nobody to help or ease the anguish. If someone is really at their wits' end, he or she may be suffering from insomnia, depression, panic attacks, or paranoia, which are making matters worse.

The message behind this card is to try and take your head out of your hands, to look up and look around so that you can take steps towards remedying whatever plagues you. The head in the hands can also symbolize a refusal to look at life—the ostrich with its head in the sand—and in this sense there are echoes of the Two of Swords, pointing to a state of paralysis or some kind of deadlock which is getting you nowhere.

the 10 of Swords

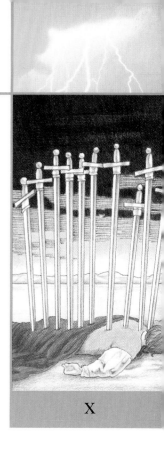

X

A figure lies face down in the earth, all ten Swords driven into his body.

In many ways this card is an equivalent to the Death card, as this figure is undeniably dead and there is nothing that can be done to bring him back to life. As with the Death card, the Ten of Swords means that something has come to a very definite end, and usually in a painful way. More often than not I have seen this card come up in the context of a relationship question, where a person is desperate to win back lost love or to keep a difficult partnership on its feet, but the sad truth is that it is over. Whether it's a relationship, a job, or any other situation, there is no going back and it is often best to let the door slam shut behind you.

However, as with all death symbolism, the flip side of the coin is rebirth. In the Ten of Swords the horizon in the background is streaked with gold as the dawn breaks, reminding us that the darkest hour is just before dawn. Rebirth imagery should never be used as a way of minimizing pain or loss, but to give us strength and hope. This is the end of something in its present state, but not the end of life.

The Ten of Swords appeared as a past card for a girl in her very early twenties. She came from a dysfunctional family and she had just moved away from her home town in order to start afresh. She felt that her relationship with her family was at an end in terms of ever developing any real closeness or intimacy and, sadly, I had to agree with her. However, I also reminded her that the Ten of Swords doesn't necessarily spell the end forever. In spite of the pain and sense of hopelessness she was feeling at present, I asked her to keep an open mind. This would mean accepting that her family was never going to be what she wanted them to be, but she could still hold the idea that some level of reconciliation might be possible in the future once she had changed her own life.

CUPS

The Cups symbolize love and our emotional lives, so these are especially important cards when dealing with relationship issues. You will deduce from the example readings in this book, and almost certainly from your own practice, that affairs of the heart are at the top of the list of the type of questions you will be asked. Even those who would not normally consider a reading will turn to divination when it comes to sorting out their love life.

Links to Astrology
Cups match the symbolism of:

Venus *The planet of love, romance, and relating.*

The Moon *Ruling our instincts, habits, and emotional needs.*

In modern times the cup is an established symbol of ritual. Cups of wine symbolize the blood of Christ in Christian services; and we raise our cups in toasts to wish health, happiness, or success. However, if we look further back into folklore, we find the symbolic connection between the cup, the element of water, and its links to the feminine world of fertility and feelings.

The suit of Cups encompasses the whole spectrum of human feelings, from hope and happiness, to loss and despair. However, it also speaks of how you feel about other things in your life and to what extent a job, a situation, or decision will bring you pleasure or pain.

IN ASTROLOGICAL TERMS

The Cups correspond to water, the element that rules feelings, instincts, and moods. The main qualities and characteristics symbolized by water can be found in the following lists of keywords and phrases:

Positive Instinctive, empathic, sympathetic, sensitive, receptive, tender-hearted, gentle, kind, protective, nurturing, compassionate, romantic, sexy, seductive, charming, enigmatic, profound, still waters run deep, artistic, poetic, fertile imagination, creative, appreciative of the arts.

Negative Impressionable, inconstant, moody, unfathomable, a wet blanket, vacillating, manipulative, deceitful, distrustful, over-concerned with privacy, paranoid, neurotic, self-pitying, victim role, timid, insincere, unfocused, addictive, over-sentimental or nostalgic.

The Cups are especially important when dealing with relationship issues.

the **Ace** of **Cups**

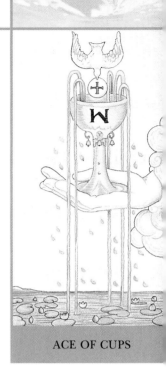

ACE OF CUPS

As with all the Aces the offering is made by a hand emerging from a cloud. In this case the hand bears an ornate cup from which five streams cascade down into a lily pond, reminding us of the symbolic link between the Cups and the element of water. A dove flies down to the Cup, holding the communion wafer in its beak.

NEW BEGINNINGS

Aces are always beginnings and the Ace of Cups symbolizes the dawning of a new chapter in your emotional life. More often than not this comes along in the shape of a powerful attraction to someone new, symbolizing the euphoric state of falling in love and creating an exciting new romantic relationship.

It can also show that you are ready to start again if you have been hurt in the past, so, if someone is single and looking for love, then you could hardly ask for a more optimistic card. However, it is worth remembering that the offering of the Cup suggests that the opportunity for love will be presented rather than actively sought. Love finds you, rather than the other way around, so this is an even more powerful card for someone who says that he or she will never love again.

YOUR HEART'S DESIRE

The Ace of Cups can also indicate the chance to embark upon a new venture or project that particularly appeals to you, something that you feel excited or passionate about. But wherever someone is looking for good fortune—whether it's a relationship, a job, a new home, and so on—there is no doubt that this is an extremely encouraging card when it comes to being offered your heart's desire.

GROWTH

The association of the Cups with the element of water also spells fertility, so this card can signal an actual pregnancy or birth. Alternatively, a new relationship or situation will grow, flourish, and prosper. Water is also powerfully linked with healing and cleansing. With the dove as a universal symbol of peace, forgiveness, and spiritual values, this is a positive card to have if you need to offer an olive branch or heal a rift. Reconciliation will lead to a fresh start.

"To medieval pagans, witches, and alchemical mystics, the cup was a universal symbol of the mother element, water—especially the waters of the sea womb that was supposed to have given birth to the earth and all that lived on it. In the Tarot, the suit of cups stood for the same water element and was replaced in later card packs by the equally maternal symbol of the heart." [17]

The Ace of Cups often shows at the beginning of a new relationship.

the **2** of **Cups**

II

A man and a woman come together, face to face. Both are young and handsome and they raise their Cups to each other.

This is quite simply the "marriage" card, showing a union and coming together of two people. It points to a very strong relationship, falling in love, getting engaged, setting the date for a wedding, or making a firm commitment. There is a rightness and simplicity about this card, reminding us that when love is right it is uncomplicated. If this card comes up in the context of a relationship, and there are no difficult cards to negate it, you can be assured that the feelings are mutual and that it will end in a strong union.

The Two of Cups came up in a reading for a friend who was in the very early stages of a relationship with someone she had known for years, someone she had always secretly wanted to marry. The Two of Cups was the outcome card in her spread, which was a delight for her and a relief and pleasure for me. It's always wonderful when you can genuinely tell someone what they are desperate to hear. Six years down the road they are still together and going strong.

the **3** of **Cups**

III

Three young women come together and form a circle as they dance with joy. As they dance they raise their Cups aloft as if toasting each other, or maybe just reveling in the pleasure of a special occasion.

This is the card of friendship and good times, which can mark anything from a great night out on the town to the longer lasting pleasure of someone's love and company. More often than not I have found that this card indicates special times of celebration, and I have seen it show for engagement, marriage, and news of a birth. But whatever the occasion, the Three of Cups is about merriment, sheer delight, and the party spirit, either in relation to our own life or on behalf of someone we care about.

Whether you are doing a reading for a man or a woman, this card can sometimes point to the value of our female friends. It can speak of that special connection created between women or the enjoyment of feminine company.

the **4** of **Cups**

IV

A young man sits with arms and legs crossed, indicating strong barriers and a lack of receptivity, and looks forlornly at the three Cups lined up in front of him. He does not notice the fourth Cup which, like the Ace, is being offered by a hand emerging from a cloud.

In stark contrast to the preceding card, the Four of this suit is about despondency. This card can mean that you are so preoccupied with your feelings for a particular person, often someone who does not return your feelings, that you miss out on other opportunities, even those which are right under your nose. The mood of this card is dis-spirited and often shows when someone is stuck in the past, obsessed with a relationship that is over, or that never really took off.

Also, look out for other contexts in which someone is suffering from a disappointment and brooding about it. There may even be some depression or pessimism, a "what's the point?" attitude, and a belief that life is against you. Other cards will help you to separate out appropriate sadness from sulking or self-pity. However, whatever the situation, the message of this card is to let go of the past, look up and take notice of other people, and to give other loves a chance.

The Four of Cups came up for a woman in her forties who was involved with a man who was still with his first wife but on the point of divorce. In this case, the Four of Cups clearly spoke of him, as he was not really ready for a new commitment. Even though his children were grown and gone, and his marriage had been over for a long time, he was preoccupied with a sense of waste. My client was not unsympathetic to his feelings, but she also felt that he didn't really appreciate how good they could be together or how much she had to offer him. In this case, there were other positive cards that painted a hopeful picture and, although the Four of Cups reminds us that affairs of the heart cannot be rushed, I felt that with time and gentle encouragement her patience would be rewarded. I learned at a later date that it was.

the **5** of **Cups**

V

The rigid figure is robed in black, head hung in sorrow, clearly suffering as he or she stands before the three Cups strewn on the ground, the water soaking away into the earth.

As with the Four of Cups, this card is also one of sadness. However, whereas the Four speaks mostly of despondency, the Five of Cups generally indicates a much deeper and often harrowing pain. I often call the Five of Cups "the grief card," as it rarely shows unless someone is in a state of mourning or is in deep distress.

In emotional terms this is a card of great loss, such as a divorce, and it usually indicates the early stages of trauma, when feelings are still raw and starting again seems like an impossible task. It is crucial to validate someone's pain when this card appears. Only then can you draw attention to the two Cups still standing upright behind the figure, symbolizing that there is still some love or happiness to be salvaged. Or the Cups can simply mean that life goes on and that we will, in time, love again.

Apart from lost love in the romantic sense, the Five of Cups can show at a time of mourning, when someone is still coming to terms with a bereavement.

the **6** of **Cups**

VI

With old buildings in the background, the country clothes of the two figures and the cups brimming with flowers, this card depicts a rural setting, suggesting innocence and simplicity.

The two figures could be either small adults or children, and this ambiguity is in itself informative. The Six of Cups often points to the past and our reminiscences—how we sometimes sentimentalize our younger years. It may indicate a need to return to simple values, or it may be that we are being over-idealistic or naïve.

In my own readings I have often found that this card speaks of an old flame making a reappearance, or someone special coming back into our lives, possibly someone we have known since childhood or at least for many years. Or it speaks of an ongoing relationship with strong roots in the past.

the 7 of Cups

A silhouetted figure gazes up at the seven Cups in the clouds, six of which hold a treasure or something to be feared, while the seventh, central card, is shrouded with a cloth.

I often refer to this as "the choice card," with the shrouded cup representing the unknown quantity that is present in all choices or decisions. We can never know everything in advance or have absolute guarantees, and there is always an element of risk.

This card suggests the need to take the risk, to commit yourself either to a relationship or to a course of action that you are still hesitant about. When this card appears it nearly always signals a state of confusion—wondering if you are hankering after the unobtainable or thinking that the grass is always greener on the other side. But the main message is that you cannot stand and stare forever. You will never know what can be achieved unless you are willing to go ahead and take the plunge.

The Seven of Cups often shows us that we need to take the plunge and make a commitment.

VII

The Seven of Cups appeared for a woman in her early forties who had, against her better instincts, stayed in a marriage that did not meet her emotional or intellectual needs. When I conveyed the message of the Seven of Cups, she said it described her perfectly—that she had been in a state of hesitation for as long as she could remember. She also said that she was nearer to taking the risk than ever before and had realized that there would never be the perfect moment for leaving. If she continued to play safe, she could miss out on finding real happiness.

the **8** of **Cups**

VIII

All eight Cups are stacked up in the foreground, none of them knocked over or concealed, yet the figure turns his back on the Cups and walks away.

I have always thought that the Eight of Cups is one of the saddest cards of the Tarot. Something special has been found and yet, for some reason, it has to be rejected. Astrologers will recognize the Sun and the Moon together in the sky, a physical impossibility, but a symbol of an eclipse. Something has been eclipsed, a light has gone out, or a shadow has fallen across that which is desired.

In terms of a relationship, there is often the context of the love being absolute and real, but the timing being disastrous.

Eclipse symbolism often indicates a third party—an eclipse is the combination of the three bodies of the Sun, Moon, and the Earth and their alignment with each other—so listen out for stories of affairs gone wrong. I have seen this card show more than once for someone who has a lover but who realizes that his or her family responsibilities have to come first. He or she decides to choose duty before the heart's desire.

The Eight of Cups came up in a spread for a woman in her fifties, and it was crossed by the Three of Swords—pain or disappointment. The heart's desire is not always a lover. This lady had bought the house of her dreams, a mountain retreat for which she had saved for many years, but as soon as she moved in she realized that, as beautiful as it was, she simply couldn't live there. She had thought she would love it, but she didn't. At the time of the reading, the house was on the market and she was looking for a place by the sea, having realized her true priority was to live by water. Fittingly, she was a Pisces.

the **9** of **Cups**

A full-figured and affluent man sits happily in the foreground of the picture. Behind him the nine Cups, all upright, are arranged in the shape of a horseshoe on a blue cloth.

This is the card of contentment, being where you want to be and sitting pretty. There is a sense of being well-fed, not just physically, but on every level, and being able to enjoy the pleasures of life.

The Nine of Cups is also known as "the wish card," so this is a lovely card to see in any spread. It indicates that you will get what you want and, furthermore, that it will live up to your expectations. This is not a case of hankering after something and then not wanting it when you get it.

The Nine of Cups, unsurprisingly, appears mostly in questions about love and relationships, and especially when a new attraction is gathering momentum and the best is yet to come. However, if it shows as a card for the present or the recent past, it is likely that someone is already enjoying new-found contentment. Love matters aside, the Nine of Cups is a wonderful omen for any heartfelt desire, such as a job or success in any other area of life.

IX

the **10** of **Cups**

A couple stand united and joyful in front of their home, while their two children play alongside them. As they behold their world, which is crowned by the ten Cups above them in the arc of a rainbow, the couple each has an arm outstretched as if to give thanks.

Whenever this card appears in a reading, I usually describe it with the words, "Cups are love, and the Ten is the best." As with the suit of Pentacles, the Ten in this suit is as good as it gets. In terms of a relationship, this card indicates living together, marriage, children, deep contentment, and long-lasting security. But for any desired goal it spells success, achievement, and celebration.

The Ten of Cups showed as the recent past for a woman who had been married for 12 years. Her husband had a very short fuse, a rigid outlook, no outside interests, and had become impossible to live with. Recently she had had a wonderful time on a business trip with a male colleague. She had had a taste of the Ten of Cups. However, she wisely acknowledged that this man was the catalyst, not the answer.

X

These cards make up the second section of the Minor Arcana. There are 16 Court cards—a King, a Queen, a Knight, and a Page for each of the four suits. These cards can describe personality traits, our own or other people's, or situations. Interpretations are offered for either possibility, along with suggestions for astrological comparisons, and anecdotes taken from my own practice.

THE COURT CARDS

4

the **Court** cards

Of the Tarot, the Court cards are probably the most difficult cards to interpret. They can be read in three ways—to represent other people, describe situations, or symbolize facets of our own nature. However, once we establish a framework, these cards are less ambiguous.

Responses and behavior

Situations tend to bear the hallmark of the people who are involved in them, and the Court cards can supply more information in terms of what we're actually dealing with, how we or other people are responding and behaving. So, when these cards appear in a spread we need to be especially open-minded and even more attentive to context. ·

Maybe it is the desire to make these cards more specific in meaning that has brought about the practice of associating each of the Court cards with physical characteristics. However, in my own experience, I have never found these cards to work in terms of representing a blond woman or a tall dark man. Neither do the Pages, Knights, and Kings always have to be men, or the Queens always have to be women. When the Court Cards describe other people, their value seems to lie in that they assist us in sketching out the *type* of person, and how we experience them in relation to ourselves.

THE QUEENS

If the client is a woman, I have often found that the Queen can act as her "significator"—the card describing the client's nature and situation, and some Tarot readers assign a Court card as a significator before beginning a reading. However, I prefer to see what comes up rather than making any conscious choice.

The Page of Cups shows someone sensitive, romantic, or artistic.

The Knight of Swords shows action, movement, and events happening quickly.

If a Queen appears with the Page, Knight, or King of the same suit, this shows a pairing and usually bodes well for relationship issues. If the Queen appears with another Court card of a different suit, there may be issues of compatibility to be addressed, and each pairing needs to be interpreted in its own right. For example, the Queen of Cups with the Knight of Swords is not an easy combination. The Knight could easily let himself ride roughshod over the Queen, not recognizing her need for empathy and gentleness, leaving her feeling crushed and wounded and leaving him feeling irritated and impatient. However, if the Queen is paired with the King of Pentacles, this would feel much more stable. This King would provide the perfect conditions for the Queen to thrive—stability, sensuality, and tolerance.

CORRELATIONS WITH ASTROLOGY

Astrology is so psychologically rich that it is helpful to make correlations between the

The Queen of Pentacles shows someone at ease and enjoying the good things of life.

Court cards and the planets and signs. These correlations are not hard and fast rules but can enhance our interpretations. As with the Minor Arcana, the suits correspond to the four elements and the three astrological signs of each element.

Whether the planet is weak or strong in a certain sign can conjure up a more detailed image. For example, the Knight of Pentacles might be described by the element of earth and then further by the planet Mars. If he is well placed he can show someone who has a true sense of purpose and who will succeed in their ambitions against all odds, just like Mars in Capricorn, Mars' sign of exaltation. If the Knight is badly placed, he may show someone who is stubborn, stuck, or bullying, just like Mars in Taurus, Mars' sign of detriment. Alternatively, he may describe someone who is exacting and cautious, or show a situation that needs such skills, like Mars in meticulous Virgo.

Letting the card speak to you as if it were a planet in a particular sign can feed your symbolic understanding and intuition. You will often find that, if the Court card depicts a person, then that person will have a Sun sign of the relevant suit. This is not an invariable rule, but I will use some examples when I refer to my own readings later in the chapter.

The King of Wands is alert, energetic, capable, and dignified—a natural leader.

Links to Astrology
Correlations are not hard and fast rules but are there to enhance our interpretations:

Pages
Mercury—the planet of youth, ideas, and communication.

Knights
Mars—the planet of war, action, and energy.

Queens
Venus—the planet of love, pleasure, and relating, and the Moon—the lady of the night who rules all things feminine and emotions.

Kings
The Sun—the light of the day, who rules all things masculine, Jupiter—the planet of knowledge and expansion, and Saturn—the planet of age, experience, and discipline.

THE PAGES

Traditionally the Pages are said to represent youth. If they stand for another person, this is most likely to be someone younger than you, but not necessarily children. A Page may represent a grown-up son or daughter who may already have their own family. The Pages can also describe people who are older than us but are immature or child-like. When the Pages represent situations, these are generally matters that are still in their early stages.

the Page of Wands

A young man holds the Wand in front of him, contemplating its buds.
He stands in a desert, with three pyramids in the background.

Links to Astrology
Mercury in Aries,
Leo, or Sagittarius.

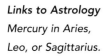

PAGE OF WANDS

AS A PERSONALITY

This is someone who is confident and resourceful. Wands correlate to the element of fire and this Page has typically fiery characteristics—energetic, creative, and positive. Fiery types tend to have warmth and enthusiasm, so this is someone who is likely to be popular, spontaneous, a self-starter, and who knows how to motivate and inspire other people. This is someone who may be coming into your life to teach you something. He or she may be adventurous, from a foreign country, or have connections overseas. If this Page is badly placed the card may speak of someone who is too impulsive, restless, or with a tendency never to finish what they start.

AS A SITUATION

The Page of Wands can indicate plans for a holiday or for new projects which require vision and creative talents. This card can also mean that news from abroad is on the way, such as a job offer overseas or news from someone who lives abroad.

The Page of Wands is nearly always someone likeable, a new friend or sometimes a lover. He showed in a reading for a young woman who had met a man during her travels and was wondering if she would see him again. The other cards suggested this was unlikely but, to soften the disappointment, I talked about the Page of Wands as someone who passes through our lives, who teaches us something or gives us a good time. However, the Page of Wands' restlessness and quest for new experiences means that this person is not necessarily a good choice of partner, as this Page is a free spirit and not ready to settle down.

the **Page** of **Pentacles**

A young man holds a pentacle aloft, balancing it delicately on his fingertips.

AS A PERSONALITY

This is someone who is thoughtful and careful. Pentacles correlate to the element of earth and this Page has typically earthy characteristics—dependable, skillful, in touch with the material world and aware of the value of money.

AS A SITUATION

The Page of Pentacles can describe the beginnings of a new project or enterprise. This card augurs well for money-making ideas of all kinds. It is not uncommon for this card to appear for someone who is in a rut and needs to make a career change, especially in terms of finding his or her true vocation.

The Page of Pentacles was crossed by the Three of Swords in a reading for a man in his sixties, painting a picture of someone causing him pain and anguish. The Page was not his son but his most valued employee, someone he loved and trusted implicitly, and with whom he also socialized in spite of a nearly 20-year age gap. In fact, he counted him as one of the people closest to him, could talk to him "about anything," and valued his ideas and input at every level. Hear how this describes the Page of Pentacles so aptly—a person younger than the client, reliable, hardworking—and how these earthy characteristics are fleshed out with the Mercury symbolism of someone who is full of ideas and conversation.

The pain and heartbreak of the Three of Swords was not because he had been let down or disillusioned but because, at the age of 46, this man had been diagnosed with terminal liver cancer. For my client this was a tragedy in both his personal and business life which, understandably, he was struggling to come to terms with.

PAGE OF PENTACLES

The Page of Pentacles is an omen for money-making ideas. It can also show the need for a career change.

Links to Astrology
Mercury in Taurus, Virgo, or Capricorn.

PAGE OF SWORDS

The three other Pages are all still and contemplative figures, whereas the Page of Swords is a card of movement. The wind lifts his hair as he strikes an aggressive pose, sword raised in both hands, as if ready to strike or charge.

AS A PERSONALITY

This is someone who is alert and sharp, but possibly somewhat unfeeling. Swords correlate to the element of air and this Page has typically airy characteristics—bright, quick, and lively. But airy types tend to let the head dominate the heart and need to learn about empathy, consideration, and the emotional consequences of their actions.

AS A SITUATION

The Page of Swords can describe things being done in too much of a hurry. Something needs to be weighed up much more carefully before you go charging into action or go on the attack. You may win the battle but lose the war and it's important to think about what you want the final outcome to be. There is a greater risk of impatience, making rash decisions, doing things for the wrong reasons, or blinding yourself to your real motivation.

The Page of Swords often represents a rather tricky character, someone who gossips or who creates trouble, either through deliberate stirring or through thoughtlessness. This is someone who does not relate or bond easily with his or her fellow human beings and he or she tends to invite dislike or suspicion. He appeared in a spread for a young woman asking about her new job, which was due to start the following week. I warned her that such a person might be among her colleagues and that she should be careful whom she befriended. I later found out that a personality clash with another woman had been so bad that my client had left the company within a month and moved elsewhere.

Links to Astrology
Mercury in Gemini, Libra, or Aquarius.

the **Page** of **Cups**

A colorful young man stands at the ocean's edge and gazes at the fish emerging from the cup that he holds in his hand.

AS A PERSONALITY

This is someone who is sensitive, romantic, or artistic. Cups correlate to the element of water, a link that is very strongly illustrated in this card, as the ocean and the fish point us directly to the symbolism of Pisces, the sign of the fishes. This Page has typically watery characteristics— imaginative, emotional, and highly receptive. There may be some naivety or tendency to daydream too much, as this person still needs to learn how to deal with the reality of the world or learn how to make their dreams materialize.

AS A SITUATION

The Page of Cups can describe something which is in the embryonic stage. The water signs are all linked with fertility or reproduction in some way. The fish emerging from the Cup can be a symbol of birth, indicating pregnancy or the conception of an idea that will prove highly productive if it is worked through. The fish can also be a symbol of rebirth for someone who is starting a new relationship and learning to get back into the world of feelings and relating.

PAGE OF CUPS

The Page of Cups can sometimes indicate a pregnancy. I sometimes do a "one card" reading for a question which is very clearly stated and which requires a simple "yes" or "no." I did such a reading for a young woman who suspected that she might be pregnant. I fanned out the cards face down as usual and asked her to choose just one, and she picked out the Page of Cups. From this one-card reading I judged that her suspicion was correct and that she was indeed expecting a baby. This was confirmed with a positive pregnancy test in the following week.

Links to Astrology
Mercury in Cancer, Scorpio, or Pisces.

THE KNIGHTS

Whereas the Pages traditionally stand for youth, the Knights represent young adults. However, the same flexibility applies as described for the Pages in that this does not dictate a prescribed age range. I have generally found that the Knights tend to stand for someone of roughly our own age, or they relate to our peers who may be younger or older than us.

the Knight of Wands

The Knight of Wands sits astride a horse. As with the Page of Wands, he is in a desert, with three pyramids in the background. This is a card of movement.

Links to Astrology
Mars in Aries, Leo, or Sagittarius.

KNIGHT OF WANDS

AS A PERSONALITY

This is someone who is energetic, adventurous, direct, and impulsive. He is similar to the Page, who also displays typically "fiery" characteristics. The Knight shares the more unpredictable fiery qualities, such as being headstrong or impractical. This person can be very exciting to be around, but he or she may not have enough grit, determination, or the means to finish what is started. In romance this is someone who can sweep you off your feet, but will he or she stick around? Again, as with the Page, look out for foreign connections, too.

AS A SITUATION

The Knight of Wands indicates challenges, educational opportunities, new ventures, or events which happen swiftly. Whatever the driving force, there is a sense of a very strong impetus here.

The Knight of Wands appeared in a spread for a woman who was a single parent of two boys, one of whom had already left home and the other was about to go to college. As it was impossible for her to secure a grant for him, she was bracing herself to fund him through a degree course for the next three years, which in effect meant putting her own life on hold during this time. However, this boy had a history of not finishing what he started and had already changed his mind several times about which course to take. The outcome card was the Three of Wands—looking out into the world and wanting to be somewhere else. I felt that he probably wasn't ready for the commitment of three years' serious study and suggested that they looked at alternatives such as a gap year.

the **Knight** of **Pentacles**

The Knight of Pentacles sits astride a sturdy black horse. He is the only Knight who is completely stationary, sitting quietly as he contemplates the Pentacle in his right hand.

AS A PERSONALITY

This is someone who is patient, steadfast, and able to stay focused on his or her goals. As with the Page of Pentacles, these are typically "earthy" characteristics. The flip side to the Pentacle when it shows as the Knight is that it can point to someone who is rather plodding, stubborn, or over-cautious. This person is not usually a self-starter or an initiator and may need to be coerced into action.

AS A SITUATION

The Knight of Pentacles generally means that there will eventually be a positive outcome to a situation which has been developing for some time, even though it may have been dragging on and threatening to end in a stalemate. Results tend not to come quickly with this card but, when they do, they are built to last and worth waiting for. If this card appears alongside others that indicate a lack of movement—for example, the Four of Pentacles or the Eight of Swords—there may be the need to use a bit more force or determination to get things going and moving in the right direction rather than just trusting in the fullness of time.

Alternatively, you may simply be facing a situation that is not worth the effort, and be banging your head against the proverbial brick wall.

The Knight of Pentacles came up in a spread for a woman in her early fifties. Other cards suggested some despondency and the Knight clearly indicated her son, who was in his late twenties, still at home, and not showing any signs of moving. Here is an example where the astrological correlation works perfectly, as her son was a Taurus, the sign of fixed earth, associated with material values and the love of creature comforts.

Money was a major issue in this situation, partly because her son said he couldn't afford to leave home, and partly because he was continually borrowing from her. The other issue was that my client felt guilty about her son, as if his inertia were somehow her fault. But whatever her role may have been in the past, the present needed to be dealt with. I pointed out that by bailing him out she was making them both feel better in the short term, but with no longer-term benefits on either side. She agreed that the situation was unhealthy and the crucial point of the reading was to show her that she was enabling his dependency. My interpretation was that her son would never leave unless pushed and that she needed to pluck up the courage to take on the fight.

KNIGHT OF PENTACLES

*Links to Astrology
Mars in Taurus,
Virgo, or Capricorn.*

KNIGHT OF SWORDS

Even more so than the Knight of Wands, the Knight of Swords is a card of action and movement. Only the front half of the horse is visible as it charges into the picture at full gallop, the Knight leaning forward and brandishing his sword in his right hand.

AS A PERSONALITY

This is someone who is capable and fearless but possibly also reckless. This Knight can create a stir wherever he or she goes, and may be highly charismatic but unreliable. He or she can be a strong ally but only for as long as it suits him or her. You need to be careful about placing your trust too readily in this person as you could easily get hurt.

AS A SITUATION

The Knight of Swords speaks of events happening quickly or completely out of the blue. There is a risk of things degenerating into chaos unless there is someone to take control.

Links to Astrology
Mars in Gemini, Libra, or Aquarius. He also has a flavor of Uranus, which co-rules Aquarius; symbolizing change, rebellion, shocks, and surprises.

The Knight of Swords came up in a spread for a woman in her late fifties. The first card of the spread was the Nine of Swords, pointing to acute anxiety. The Knight of Swords described the coming situation, and her dilemma revolved around the husband of a recently deceased friend. He was unable to cope and was urging her and her husband to come and live with him. Having just retired, she was poised to start living the rest of her life to the full and the future was looking bright. She was struggling with the ethical dilemma of putting her own needs and plans first or shelving them in order to help this man. I urged caution and for her to look at all the alternatives before offering up the rest of her life as a sacrifice.

The Knight of Swords can easily sweep you off your feet.

the **Knight** of **Cups**

The Knight of Cups is a peaceful card. The Knight holds forth the cup as he quietly moves forward on a gray horse, who is clearly docile.

AS A PERSONALITY

This is someone who is loving, sincere, and sensitive. These are typically "watery" characteristics and the Knight of Cups describes a person whose heart rules his head. Traditionally, the Knight of Cups stands for a proposal of marriage and I have frequently seen this card show as a good old-fashioned suitor, the original "knight in shining armor," someone who will make a proposal or who wants a genuine and committed relationship. The flip side of the coin is that he or she may not be so good at the practicalities of life or be really prepared for the reality of a relationship, especially once it has gone past the honeymoon stage. If the card is badly placed it can warn of someone who is unable to offer you what you really want in spite of your desire for him or her.

AS A SITUATION

The Knight of Cups can stand for all kinds of proposals, from a business offer to ideas and plans that particularly appeal to you. If this card appears alongside others that suggest difficulties, then the offers need to be checked out in more detail.

KNIGHT OF CUPS

The Knight of Cups crossed the Nine of Swords at the center of the Celtic Cross spread in a reading for a woman in her thirties. The Nine of Swords points to despair and anxiety, so this looked like a case of unrequited love, which my client immediately confirmed. She was desperate for this man's love, but I wondered if she were also desperate to get married and whether this was a question of finding the cap and making it fit. She admitted that this was partly true and that, with sisters and friends all paired off, the need for a committed relationship was becoming stronger and stronger. Yet she had attached herself to a man who, although of a caring nature, which the Knight of Cups describes, was not in love with her. He had also told her from the outset that he did not want to get married, as he already had a divorce behind him, but of course she held on to the hope that he would change his mind.

One of the hallmarks of a spread that hits the mark is rich symbolism that can be read in more than one way. Note how the Knight of Cups in conflict with the Nine of Swords speaks so clearly of the situation from both angles. Here is both the man's attitude and past experience, and her frustrated desire. Other cards in the spread gave no indication that the situation would improve, so I had to judge that this man would never be her knight in shining armor.

Links to Astrology Mars in Cancer, Scorpio, or Pisces. He also has a flavor of Neptune, the planet that co-rules Pisces, symbolizing the imagination, dreams, redemption, escapism, and the "urge to merge."

THE QUEENS

The Queens generally signify the women in our lives, but this is not a hard and fast rule. The most important thing is to look at the type of person the Queen describes and the role the person is playing before we assume the person is female. In terms of age, the Queens can represent the whole spectrum. They can also represent parents or people in authority.

the Queen of Wands

A confident woman sits on a throne and surveys her surroundings. The throne is engraved with lions, a black cat sits at her feet, and the Queen holds a sunflower in her hand.

Links to Astrology
The Moon or Venus in Leo or in the other fire signs of Aries or Sagittarius.

AS A PERSONALITY

This is someone who is capable, resourceful, strong, and dignified. He or she is the center of his or her universe and may represent the key person in a family and the one who holds it all together. This Queen can represent anyone from a parent to an efficient and motivated business person. This person is a natural leader with excellent organizational skills. The flip side is that this person may also have the more difficult characteristics associated with the fire sign of Leo, such as fierce pride, a domineering attitude, or a tendency to boss other people around. This Queen may have difficulty with delegation, as she believes that nobody can do things as well as she can. At her most powerful, she may also be psychic.

AS A SITUATION

The Queen of Wands speaks of matters being well in hand, because someone has a good grasp of the overall picture.

QUEEN OF WANDS

> **The Queen of Wands** appeared in a reading for a woman in her early forties, who was a Leo. Her Moon sign was Scorpio, which is associated with issues of control. This difficult astrological combination was reflected in a layout where the Queen was flanked by the Nine and Ten of Wands. The woman's main issue was that she felt oppressed by the demands of her husband and ten-year-old child, who were extremely needy and dependent on her. She had become bitterly resentful. Before discussing how she could make changes, I asked her to consider how she had got into this position. Was it her need to be needed? She was now backed into a corner and clearly something had got to give.

the Queen of Pentacles

A richly dressed woman sits on an intricately carved throne beneath a bower of roses, contemplating the pentacle which she holds gently in her lap.

QUEEN OF PENTACLES

AS A PERSONALITY

The Queen of Pentacles' throne is set in a field, which is lush with flowers and vegetation, presenting a picture of fertility and abundance. Here is a clear correlation between the pentacles and the element of earth. This is someone who is sitting pretty, at ease with her surroundings and enjoying the good things of life in the land of plenty. This person is steady, nurturing, constructive, and appreciative. There are strong similarities with the Empress in the Major Arcana, who also represents a figure very close to nature and at home in the material world.

AS A SITUATION

The Queen of Pentacles indicates that everything in the garden is rosy. When this card appears it points to great stability, either in the financial or emotional sense, or that greater security is coming and circumstances will improve.

The Queen of Pentacles

appeared in a spread for a woman in her late thirties who lived in a beautiful house in the hills with spectacular views of the sea. This was a house that she and her husband had literally built from scratch. She told wonderful stories about living close to the land. She felt enormously fortunate and said that she had never expected to end up somewhere so beautiful and with so much to be grateful for. She now kept bees so she was both literally and metaphorically living in the land of milk and honey.

Physically she was wonderfully described by the Queen of Pentacles —exuding good health and vitality.

Links to Astrology
The Moon or Venus in Taurus, Virgo, or Capricorn.

QUEEN OF SWORDS

An austere woman sits on a gray throne, presenting a side profile. Her expression is somewhat stern and forbidding as she looks straight ahead, her sword held vertically in her right hand in a challenging pose.

AS A PERSONALITY

This is someone who is a tough and independent character, a person who is ready to take a hard line and to fight for what he or she wants. She or he is fair, shrewd, logical, and matter-of-fact. Traditionally, this Queen is a widow, but she can also represent someone who is divorced or separated, or someone who has been alone for a long time and who does not bond easily with other people. In spite of the hard edges and tough exterior, this person often indicates someone who is just plain lonely and shy, and who feels that she has no choice but to take on the world singlehandedly. In order to make the world safer and more manageable, there is a tendency to put a lot of energy into staying in control and to avoid taking risks of any kind.

AS A SITUATION

The Queen of Swords can indicate tough opposition and hard bargains to be driven. Results will probably not come easily and it may be a case of being up against rigid rules or some kind of red tape that is difficult to cut through. Matters are likely to be dealt with very fairly but strictly by the book, and with no room for sentiment or personal feelings.

Links to Astrology
The Moon or Venus in Gemini, Libra, or Aquarius.

The Queen of Swords appeared in a reading for a woman in her early thirties, with the Queen crossing the Ten of Pentacles at the center of the Celtic Cross. Her Sun sign was Taurus, but the suit of the element of air correlated to her Moon sign, which was Libra, the sign of partnership. She was making great strides in her career, earning plenty of money, and came from a loving, wealthy, and supportive family, all of which is symbolized by her Sun in earthy Taurus and by the Ten of Pentacles, the card of prosperity and family stability. She had just bought a new home, but her life was being spoiled by loneliness. There was no one to share it with, and the Queen of Swords in conflict speaks clearly of this sense of isolation.

I concentrated on how she may have become like the Queen of Swords and how this was working against her. Giving in to cynicism or bitterness, or concealing her vulnerability through fear or pride would simply perpetuate the problem. I also suggested that she needed to take other measures to relieve her loneliness rather than fixating on the idea of a partner. She needed to challenge the belief that the "right person" would make it all OK. Positive change generally starts within.

the Queen of Cups

A young fair-haired woman sits on a throne, gazing intently at the cup that she holds in both hands. The throne is placed at the water's edge and is adorned with cherubs. Notice how this cup is larger and far more ornate than the cups depicted in the rest of the suit.

AS A PERSONALITY

This is someone who has a romantic nature, with big dreams and a fertile imagination. She or he is, in many ways, the complete antithesis to the Queen of Swords, who clearly lets her head rule her heart. The Queen of Cups is the opposite and lives in the world of feelings. She may represent someone who is falling in love, starry-eyed, and full of wonderment in a magical world. This Queen is sympathetic, creative, idealistic, and possibly naïve. If she appears with difficult cards, she may represent someone who is out of touch with reality. Or she can represent someone whose dreams have never gone beyond castles in the air. There may be a need to separate fact from fantasy.

AS A SITUATION

The Queen of Cups indicates fruitful ideas but not much viability. A reality check is a must, as some projects or a relationship may prove to be ultimately unfeasible.

QUEEN OF CUPS

The Queen of Cups appeared in a difficult spread for a woman who was approaching her 40th birthday. She had been married for 18 years and had two children who were in their mid-teens. Although it was a successful marriage in many ways, her big issue was that her husband had never been able to meet her emotional needs. He was terrified of any kind of display of feelings, particularly anything connected to pain or hurt. Her dissatisfaction with her marriage had reached an all-time high, not least because she had met someone to whom she was emotionally, sexually, and intellectually attracted. She was also hatching some business ideas in order to gain more financial independence.

Around the age of 40 we experience the Uranus half return. Uranus, the planet of sudden change or rebellion, has an 80-year cycle and reaches its half-way point in our horoscope around this time. It is often referred to as the astrological mid-life crisis, a time for breaking out and doing things that we have never done before it is too late. As far as the reading went, my role was to draw attention to the Queen of Cups, to question her as to whether she had really thought things through. She needed to find out if her attraction to the new man was mutual and if he would be available. Was he really what she wanted? There were a lot of different issues to work through before she made any final decisions.

Links to Astrology
The Moon or Venus in Cancer, Scorpio, or Pisces.

THE KINGS

Traditionally the Kings represent older people but, again, I have never found that they fit neatly into a fixed age bracket. They often signify someone who is older than ourselves but, equally, they can be parents, professional figures, or people who are mature for their years or who hold a position of authority. Often, if a King appears in a reading for a man, it will act as his "significator," that is, the card will describe his own nature or particular situation.

the King of Wands

A confident man sits upright on a throne that is adorned with lion motifs, holding the Wand upright before him. As with his counterpart, the Queen of Wands, there is a clear correlation with the sign of Leo.

Links to Astrology
Either the Sun, Jupiter, or Saturn in Leo or in the fire signs of Aries or Sagittarius.

AS A PERSONALITY

This is someone who is alert, energetic, capable, and dignified, all of which are positive qualities associated with the astrological sign of Leo. Here is a natural leader, someone who tends to command respect but also liking and affection. I have generally found him to represent someone who is the source of great inspiration and motivation, such as a dedicated teacher or an enlightened boss. He may be somewhat overbearing at times, but his heart is in the right place, he is worth listening to, and is worth having on your side. The King of Wands has a small black lizard sitting at his feet, just as the Queen of Wands has a black cat. Again, there are magical connotations, and this King can represent someone who has excellent intuition and insights, bordering on the psychic. You can seek out and trust his advice.

AS A SITUATION

The King of Wands indicates that matters are well in hand and that those who are in control have both ability and vision. In some cases enthusiasm, inspiration, and intelligence may compensate for a lack of practical experience.

> **The King of Wands** appeared in a spread for a woman who had just returned to full-time education in her early thirties. She was in the final year of her BA in Literature and was thriving on it. She could hardly believe how well she had done and how much studying had enriched her life. Without hesitation she identified the King of Wands as her personal tutor, who had been a constant source of inspiration and encouragement.

KING OF WANDS

An opulent figure sits on a throne almost completely covered by his flowing robes, which are decorated with bunches of grapes on the vine. One hand rests on the Pentacle on his knee and the other holds a scepter. The top of the throne has a bull's head on either side and there are clear correlations with Taurus, the sign of fixed earth.

KING OF PENTACLES

AS A PERSONALITY

As with his counterpart, the Queen of Pentacles, this is a picture of fertility and abundance. This is someone who is dependable, responsible, and supportive. He or she is well established and usually well off, and the epitome of stability and security. This King has a steady and practical approach to life and needs a good reason for doing something rather than acting on impulse. He is as solid as a rock, the kind of person we would seek out in a crisis, especially for financial or practical help. This King is a provider, exuding gravitas and authority, and may represent a parent, a successful business person, a bank manager, or a benefactor of some kind. The flip side of the coin is that this person may have forgotten or have never known what it is like to be without, and does not always share out his good fortune or practice generosity.

AS A SITUATION

The King of Pentacles indicates that matters are extremely promising and well organized. Whoever is at the helm has everything under control and knows exactly what to do. This card augurs well for business ventures of all kinds and points to matters being highly productive and lucrative.

The King of Pentacles and the King of Wands both appeared side by side in a reading for a woman in her early fifties. I asked her if there were two important men in her life and she said she was in her second marriage, but still on excellent terms with her first husband. Her current husband was clearly identifiable as the King of Wands. He was a Sagittarian, with a huge amount of energy and enthusiasm for life, who approached everything with a great sense of adventure and a wonderful sense of humor. He brought her out of herself and they traveled extensively together. Her first husband fitted the symbolism of the King of Pentacles perfectly—a man who had started from scratch and built up his own business. He would never be short of money and still encouraged her to come to him if she ever needed help. She described him as "a very powerful man, and very supportive." However, the marriage had floundered early on as, although he could fulfil her material needs, her emotional needs had always remained unsatisfied.

Links to Astrology
Either the Sun, Jupiter, or Saturn in Taurus, Virgo, or Capricorn.

KING OF SWORDS

A stern figure sits bolt upright on his throne, his sword held aloft in his right hand. As with all of the Court cards in the Swords suit, the setting is cold and crisp, with blue skies, white clouds, and sparse vegetation in the surrounding landscape.

AS A PERSONALITY

This is someone who is fair, logical, controlled, and strict, sometimes rather forbidding. His strongest asset is a razor-sharp mind, and this King represents someone who is analytical, efficient, and of above average intelligence. Emotions are not allowed to cloud his judgment and he often represents a professional figure, such as a solicitor or a consultant. In this respect he is a good person to have on your side, but his clinical approach to life could have disastrous consequences in personal relationships.

In emotional terms, this King can be like his counterpart, the Queen of Swords, and can represent someone who is cut off from his needs or feelings, someone who uses cynicism and fierce independence as a way of warding off intimacy. This King is likely to be unresponsive or distant, and engaging this person at an intimate level can be an uphill struggle. If this card comes up in a spread as a partner, you will almost certainly encounter clients, invariably women, who are in an acute state of frustration at the lack of love, compassion, or empathy. If this King depicts a character who is against you, then you have a very tough adversary.

AS A SITUATION

The King of Swords tells you that you need a rational approach. Expectations need to be realistic, and the importance of protecting your needs should not be overlooked. You need to think with your head rather than be guided by your heart.

The King of Swords came up in a spread for a girl of 21 who was working in a holiday resort, her first job since leaving college. It was a reading in which she was determined to "give nothing away" and my attempts to engage her were met with stony resistance. I suggested that she was having a problem relating to her boss and she asked me if this person was a man or a woman. I felt strongly that it was a man, but I also explained that it was the type of person that was most important. I described this person as someone who was strict, who stuck to the book and wouldn't bend the rules, who was probably difficult to appeal to at a personal level and who treated her as "staff" rather than as an individual. I then moved on to other issues, but she said at the end of the reading that the King of Swords described her male boss "to a T."

Links to Astrology
Either the Sun, Jupiter, or Saturn in Gemini, Libra, or Aquarius.

the **King** of **Cups**

Whereas the Queen of Cups sits at the water's edge, the King of Cups is totally surrounded by water, his throne adrift on a raft. The Queen is shown gazing at her cup but the King is pictured looking out far into the distance.

AS A PERSONALITY

This is someone who is dreamy but rather uncertain, imaginative but not necessarily focused. The King is adrift on his raft and is literally "all at sea," either regarding a particular situation or relationship, or regarding his own direction or purpose in life. This person is likely to be meditative and sensitive at best, wilfully self-deceptive at worst. The real world may be too much for this King and it may be difficult for him or her to find a niche. The ocean symbolizes the sea of emotion and there is a sense of this person floating through life at the mercy of the tides. I have also found that this King often represents someone who is cut off from his own feelings and who has difficulty empathizing with others.

AS A SITUATION

The King of Cups shows that matters have yet to take proper shape and form. The details are unclear or in a muddle. Dreams and schemes may be seductive but of little substance at the end of the day.

The King of Cups appeared in a spread for a woman in her forties, crossing the Hermit at the center of the Celtic Cross. Her son was in prison on drugs charges and had another year to serve. The loneliness and angst was hard for them to bear, but her outcome card was the Three of Cups— celebration—so I was able to predict a happy ending.

The most difficult aspect of this "watery" person is that the pressures of life can lead to escapism. In turn, this can lead to a collapse of boundaries and an "urge to merge" symbiosis that we see in the early stages of falling in love. The drive to experience such altered states of consciousness can manifest in alcohol or drug addiction.

KING OF CUPS

Links to Astrology
The Sun, Jupiter, or Saturn in Cancer, Scorpio, or Pisces.

The King of Cups can be dreamy and imaginative but unfocused, literally adrift in his or her life.

Not only do we have to interpret the meaning of the cards, but the nature of the reader-client relationship demands that we also learn how to wear the therapist's hat. This section addresses the sort of issues that arise when we start doing readings for other people and illustrates how a powerful reading is one that addresses the client's true needs and issues.

BECOMING A CONSULTANT

HOBBY OR PROFESSION

Many people enjoy the Tarot as a hobby. Turning your hobby into your profession is a big step; for some it happens gradually and naturally, while for others it is a conscious decision. Either way, becoming a consultant can at first be a daunting prospect, but you don't have to be an expert in order to take the plunge.

Becoming a consultant means that you do readings for people outside of your family and circle of friends or colleagues. In terms of developing your Tarot skills, the sooner you start doing readings for others the better. Hands-on, personal experience is the best teacher in the world. However, it is essential to recognize that the client is of utmost importance, so you must familiarize yourself with the sorts of issues that are likely to arise within consultations. This chapter offers some guidelines for setting up a practice and learning how to wear the therapist's hat.

STARTING OUT

When you first begin you will almost certainly learn more from your clients than they will from you. But we all have to start somewhere, and there is no harm in letting clients know that they are part of your "apprenticeship." You are unlikely to be short of willing guinea pigs, especially as you will probably start by doing readings for free or for a nominal sum.

It is important, however, to start charging a professional fee as soon as possible, so you put a value on what you do. Nine times out of ten the client will also attach more value to the reading. A professional fee speaks of confidence in what you have to offer, the client's confidence in you, and your shared confidence in the reading. Not charging is a way of avoiding being judged. Fear of failure and of ending up with a dissatisfied

Privacy

Whether you are practicing from home or from rented space, it is vital to secure privacy. For the client there is nothing worse than the possibility of being overheard. Any risk of others listening to such a private matter will sabotage the reading before it has begun. As the reader, we are the recipient of another person's deepest concerns or secrets. This puts us in a privileged position and it is essential to create a space that is safe and conducive to intimate conversation.

It is also annoying for you and the client to be interrupted, especially when the consultation is in full flow, so minimize the chances of distractions. If there is a phone in the room, make sure it is either on answer machine or unplugged. If there are other people around, make sure that your door is closed with a "Do Not Disturb" sign clearly displayed.

You will find more information on the ideal work space in the next chapter.

customer, is natural. I still get nervous before seeing a new client and I'd be worried if I didn't! But we need to remind ourselves that, as in any kind of counseling, we are not there to "fix" the client's problems. We do not have a magic wand and it would be arrogant to think that we did. What is important is the conversation, what the client says, how you offer your interpretations and how you make the reading a meaningful experience for both of you.

CONFIDENTIALITY AND ETHICS

At some point in your consultation you may need to reassure your client that, whatever he or she divulges, it will go no further. As a practicing Tarot reader you will hear it all—I have dealt with everything from infidelity to incest—and these are clearly highly sensitive issues that your client would probably not speak of in any other circumstances. I have practiced in big cities like London and Cairo, and also in a small Greek village, but no matter how large or small your community, the same rules must apply.

Hand in hand with confidentiality goes the question of your own ethical principles and mores. These have to be suspended if you take up any profession that leads you into the world of counseling. You have to be prepared for anything to surface and you may hear things that bemuse or shock you. If your client thinks that you are sitting in judgment of him or her, your client will snap shut like the proverbial clam, and rightly so. It may be that the client has come to you precisely because he or she feels unable to talk to anyone else and, whatever our personal opinion may be, a consultation is neither the time nor place to air it. When wearing the therapist's hat, we must respond rather than react because the job of the reader is not to formulate a view but to locate the symbolism of the client's story in the cards or the horoscope.

It is important not to lose sight of the most essential matter, which is your client, so you must thoroughly familiarize yourself with the sorts of issues that are likely to arise.

THE **CONSULTATION** IN **PRACTICE**

Probably the most important skill of the consultant is the ability to listen. Your mind may be leaping to immediate and even wholly accurate interpretations as a story unfolds, but nothing is more important than letting the client speak. If you can listen to someone you will almost certainly find that the symbolism of the reading becomes clearer and your analytical understanding deeper.

You also will give your client the chance to talk of what really matters to him or her. Herein lie the therapeutic benefits of a reading and, although this happens infrequently, on more than one occasion I have pushed the cards to one side in order to make the necessary space for counseling, the "talking cure."

VALIDATE

To validate means to acknowledge that this is how your client really feels. The key word here is empathy. Any hint of a negative reaction, such as disbelief or ridicule, will have disastrous consequences and is a sure-fire way of alienating your client rather than inviting his or her trust. Be patient. A vital factor of validation is not to go straight into solution-finding mode. Your client needs to know that you can identify with what he or she is saying but you don't have to go over the top—I was once so moved by a client's story that I dissolved into tears and she ended up trying to comfort me. Since then I have learned the importance of bearing the client's pain when listening to traumatic stories. Quite often, very little needs to be said. I may say something like "That must have been awful for you," but generally the act of careful listening is enough to create the vital empathic link before moving on.

EXPLORE

To look further at an issue or feeling is a continuation of validating your client's experience, but in more detail. At this stage the reader needs to be more analytical—"What" is this? becomes "Why" is this? In a Tarot reading the exploration starts with drawing out the symbolism for the client, and you can refer back to the chapters covering the individual cards to find examples of this in the readings quoted. Don't be afraid to speak of "heavy" symbolism, such as Swords or transits of the outer planets. This kind of validation

What does the client want?

It is often helpful to ask yourself, "What does this client want?" If the answer to this question is clearly counseling, especially if the person is not engaging at a symbolic level, then the cards or the horoscope may simply act as a springboard into the conversation—the key to a door that would otherwise remain locked.

More usually, though, you will find that a consultation is peppered with therapeutic moments as issues and feelings emerge. The cards or horoscope are not pushed aside but tend to go in and out of focus as they alternate between the foreground and background of the conversation. A helpful response pattern to a client's particular issue or feeling is: validate > explore > resolve.

usually comes as a relief to your client and you will hear comments such as, "Thank God, I'm not going mad then." In the following chapter you will find more detailed information on how to handle readings, how to offer and discuss your interpretations and say what you see.

RESOLVE

Most readings are not about fortune-telling but about seeking guidance and meaning. However, we cannot often hope for the ideal outcome of resolution within one reading. Although Tarot readers can learn a lot from the world of psychotherapy, we are not therapists in the strictest sense. However, there are times when readers have no choice but to take up the role of therapist. One of the main factors that separate these two disciplines is the time factor. In therapy there are repeat appointments, sometimes over a long period of time, during which clients will unravel and "unpack" their own issues and at their own pace. Readings are at the other end of the scale, as most of them are one-off appointments.

CHOICES

To be a Tarot reader is to hold a mirror up to the human condition, but this does not mean that we can solve everyone's problems, have all the answers, and tie up all the loose ends. If only. But usually the conversation itself is therapeutic and your client will go away with plenty to think about. Ideas and coping strategies will often emerge naturally, even if there are no obvious solutions. If someone is floundering then make suggestions, but

Resistance

As with all relationships, some clients will be easier to talk to than others. Some will readily explore their issues with you and engage quickly with the idea of symbolism, while others will be quiet, distant, or inarticulate. A natural impulse with those who are non-communicative is to fill the gap by doing all the talking yourself, but this is an impulse worth curbing. Don't work overtime to draw someone out. Simple questions, such as "How does that make you feel?" and then allowing some silence for the response can be highly effective and point you both in the right direction.

don't issue directives. I often use prompts, such as "Have you considered...?" or "What about..?" I also like to raise the issue of options and choices as this challenges the unhelpful idea that our problems are fated or that we are stuck with them. Often just a recognition of choice can act as a powerful catalyst for change.

TREAD CAREFULLY

Whatever form resistance may take, it is always worth asking yourself, "What is this telling me?" Apart from resistance to engaging with you, you may sometimes meet with resistance to your interpretations or your efforts to move the client on. What do you do? The first rule is to tread carefully, as this is where the worlds of readings and therapy are more likely to collide than overlap. To tackle someone's reluctance to own something can be invasive and damaging. Recognize his or her truth and don't get into a fight as this will not be beneficial for either of you. You want to engender less resistance, not more. Accept that maybe it is the

Self-defense
Resistance can also serve a therapeutic purpose. If someone is unwilling or unable to let go of his or her defenses, this may be for a good reason. He or she is not ready and will be vulnerable if those defenses are dismantled.

wrong truth or interpretation at this stage. Interpretations are very close to opinions and we must remember that they represent *a* truth, not necessarily *the* truth.

CHALLENGING

To what extent you feel able to challenge a person's view or opinions will depend on the individual reading. The golden rule is: if in doubt, don't. Use your common sense and your intuition and you will soon develop a feel for how much someone is ready to hear or change.

On some occasions, however, a direct interjection can work wonders. In analytical language this is sometimes called "stormtrooping"—the moment when you recognize someone's self-deception, but you go in anyway. This is especially effective with minor resistance when you

are pretty sure that the client doesn't believe what he or she is saying. We all have a "script" around our self-image but we sometimes forget that it needs continual rewriting and updating. Language that gives away our script is usually negative and often includes "always" or "never," such as "I am always broke" or "I can never find the right partner." Whenever I hear this kind of language I challenge it.

EXPECTATIONS

I have already mentioned that Tarot readers do not have magic wands or quick-fix remedies. I prefer to quickly dispel any mistaken links with natural clairvoyance—a comparison explored in chapter one.

In the introduction I discussed how the Tarot reader takes up a threefold role: of

Rewriting your script

One young woman asked me about a man she had met while traveling and then announced that she wasn't sure about "relationship stuff" anyway and wasn't "really bothered" if he got in touch again. This was an obvious contradiction, so I looked her straight in the eye and said, "Aren't you?" She hesitated, but her sheepish grin told me those two words had broken the possibility of any collusion between us. I gently added, "From where I'm sitting it feels as if you are bothered, but maybe you're telling yourself that you're not so as to avoid the pain of it not happening."

You might ask, why not just answer the question from the reading? Will she see this man again, yes

or no? The question was answered from the reading, and it was in fact a "no," but to stop there would amount to fortune-telling. The real power of this reading was to connect my client with her own denial. My question seized the psychological moment and asked her to own her true desire rather than splitting off from it, even if that true desire could not be gratified. The value of such moments is the connection with truth, with our authentic selves, and the real reasons for our beliefs or behavior. This young woman's script was, "If you commit to men they always leave you." Learning how to rewrite our scripts takes us off the treadmill of denial and sets us on the path to self-development and awareness.

diviner, interpreter, and therapist rolled into one. Getting to grips with the symbolism of the Tarot, learning how to interpret what you see in the cards in conjunction with locating what you hear from your client, are the fundamental tools of your craft. You will learn something new from every reading and build up a storehouse of experience.

When it comes to the tricky position of being a temporary therapist, having therapy yourself or doing a short-term counseling course is well worth investing in. When it comes to learning counseling skills, there is no substitute for being in the hot seat yourself.

DRAWING A BLANK

Probably the biggest fear of any Tarot reader is that you will draw a total blank. This is not an unknown phenomenon, but has happened to me only three times during the last 15 years, once with a horoscope and twice with the Tarot cards. If this happens you must tell your client. On those occasions I ended the consultation and refused payment. I believe that these "non"-readings happen for a reason. Thankfully, most consultations have their fair share of rewarding moments.

On that note, the readings I enjoy least are those where there is no real issue to address. When someone has reached an impasse in his or her life but has not yet caught sight of the next stage, he or she can appear vague and will often present an empty page on which he or she wants you to write. Again, it is not the role of the Tarot reader to pull rabbits out of hats.

A reading to learn from

I vividly remember doing a reading for a woman in her fifties. She said nothing when she sat down next to me and, in a non-hostile way, resisted my attempts at preliminary conversation. This is not uncommon as most clients want to hear what you have to say before he or she volunteers any information. However, her body language revealed that she was very tense and I suspected that she had never had a reading before and didn't know what to expect. I sensed that she wanted me to get straight to the point so, when the Three of Swords showed as her recent past, I said, "You've had a heartbreak," and she smiled and nodded.

This was a perfect example of how validating someone's experience can be highly therapeutic. Simply acknowledging the pain, rather than giving a long description of the card, got the reading off to a flying start. The ensuing cards painted a very positive picture, and I was able to illustrate how her divorce would lead her to a totally new life in which she would get back to being her true self. Also, the money disputes that were ongoing would be settled in her favor.

This was a very quick reading because she didn't want to know anything else. In fact, it was so quick that I fell into the trap of offering her a discount, feeling guilty that she had taken up so little of my time when I was far more used to clients trying to spin out readings. But she simply laid the full amount on my table, gave me a big smile, and left with a spring in her step. All the tightness had disappeared and she looked like a different woman.

This was a very powerful reading for her, and also for me, because it reminded me that the time a reading takes is irrelevant. The true value of a consultation lies in the exchanges that take place and in both the reader and the client being alive to that which is revealed. What is said is more important than how long it takes to say it.

This section deals with the practical details of doing readings. You will find suggestions for preparation, how to organize your work space, and how to conduct a reading from start to finish. You will also find examples of simple spreads that are quick and easy to learn and use.

6

READINGS IN PRACTICE

PREPARATION GUIDELINES

In terms of preparation, the most important factor lies in your physical and mental readiness both for yourself and for your client. Your client's appointment must be as important to you as it is to him or her. And don't forget that greeting and meeting your client is an important part of the consultation.

There is a school of thought that says that your Tarot cards should be bought for you as a gift. While this is a lovely idea it is by no means essential. I bought my first pack myself 15 years ago and I am still using it. The cards are old, battered, and dog-eared but I wouldn't part with them for the world. I like to think that they are somehow imbued with the experience of all the stories they have unfurled and I love the sense of connection and familiarity I feel every time I get them out and handle them in readiness for a new reading.

Looking after your cards is a ritual and is a vital part of your craft. Tradition says that they should always be wrapped in a square of silk, preferably black or purple, which doubles up as the cloth on which to lay the cards for a reading. I keep my cards in a square of purple silk and then in a drawstring, plain cotton bag.

The cards should never be removed from their wrapping except for a reading or for a learning exercise. Never allow other people to play with them out of curiosity, and never leave them lying around as if they were ordinary playing cards. If I want to remember a reading, I write it down straight away so that the cards can then be put away. Treat your cards with love, respect, reverence, and awe for they will always be one of your most magical possessions.

It is important to keep your Tarot cards wrapped up and out of the way when they are not being used.

YOUR WORK SPACE

Like many other readers in my time, I have done readings over café tables, on trains, lying on beds, on beaches, squashed into corners, and so on, so I am now talking about the ideal work space.

In terms of your general setup, the most important thing to be aware of is how basic body language can influence the success of your consultation. Easy chairs may be fine for therapy, but for a Tarot reading you need upright chairs and an uncluttered work surface. Avoid sitting opposite your client, as this is a confrontational and over-authoritative pose, with the table as a barrier between you. I always sit alongside my client so that neither of us has to look at the cards from an angle or upside down.

PREPARATION

Most important is your physical and mental readiness for yourself and for your client. Think back to the last time you went for a consultation of any kind and remember how you felt. Were you nervous, excited, apprehensive, shy? Were you unsure of what to expect? Did you understand what was going on or did you feel stupid and have questions that you didn't like to ask? Remember that your client will, to a greater or lesser extent, be in this state of apprehension or excitement and, no matter how many readings you may have done, it may well be the first time for your client.

The client's appointment should be equally important to both the reader and the client. If your client arrives to find you on the phone, still clearing up, or hunting around for things, he or she will be disappointed or annoyed, and rightfully so. Your client needs to know that you are ready and waiting, so make sure that the moment of greeting and welcoming is an important part of the consultation.

In terms of being mentally prepared you simply need to be uncluttered. Whatever is going on in your own life needs to be set aside so that you can concentrate on your client and engage fully with his or her issues. You also need to feel at your sharpest, and I never book clients for a day when I have something big planned for the night before. I also don't like to do too many readings in a row. I know other readers who can carry

A feminine craft

It seems timely to add that, in my own practice, approximately 90 percent of readings are for women. No doubt you will have already deduced this from the example readings in the previous chapters, and I would imagine that it is the same for most consultants in this field. This is because the realm of divination is largely lunar, or feminine, in its nature. It belongs to the night world of instincts, feelings, nuances, shadows, and receptivity. That which is masculine is solar in nature, belonging to the day world when life is visible and obvious. Symbolism, by definition, is rarely obvious and always open to interpretation.

on for hours without showing any signs of flagging, but personally I end up feeling drained. It makes sense to know your own most effective working hours and also your own cut-off point.

I also read more effectively if my work area is clean and devoid of anything not directly linked to the reading. I have my cards, water, clock, paper, and pen for myself and for my client, and the all-important box of tissues. Tears can flow incredibly quickly and freely when you are dealing with sensitive issues or with someone in a vulnerable state.

GETTING **STARTED**

The Tarot readers I know all work in different ways. As with any craft it is a question of developing your own technique, your own systems, and finding out what works best for you. The only golden rule is consistency. In other words, once you find what works best for you, then stick to it and never vary it. In this way you create your own rituals.

Shuffling the Pack
The client does not need to be an expert shuffler. The important thing is for him or her to handle the cards.

A few minutes of small talk eases tension and acts as a "warmer." Whether you talk about the weather, your client's journey, or the pictures on the wall is irrelevant. In this way, meeting a client is a cameo of meeting any other person for the first time. You start with trivia and then move on to deeper and more personal issues. How quickly a new friendship or any relationship develops depends a great deal on how effectively you are able to peel away each other's layers, and this can take anything from moments to years. With a client, however, you've got probably less than an hour, which goes some way to explaining why the client/consultant relationship can be so intense.

During the introductory chit-chat I take my cards out of their bag, unwrap them, and lay the silk cloth on the table in front of us. In order to move on I always ask my client if he or she has ever had a reading before of any kind. If the answer is yes, I then ask what kind of reading, how long ago, was it interesting, was it what they expected, and so on. If the answer is no, I move straight into explaining how I work.

THE READING
Many Tarot readers will start by asking the client for specific questions but personally I have never found this an effective way of working. Not everyone has a specific issue, and those who do are often, and understandably, reluctant to give it away. They want the reader to see it first. As I stated earlier, I prefer to do readings for people I know nothing about, as going in "blind" generally makes for a much more powerful reading, both for the reader and for the client.

I explain that I always start with a general spread just to see what comes up, adding that the main issues mostly show up straight away. However, if there are any matters that do not arise in the general spread, we can then go on to lay other spreads for particular questions, so nothing need be unanswered.

Bear in mind that most people's concentration will waver and break after listening to someone for 15–20 minutes. For this reason I like to get the conversation going as quickly as possible, to move from a monologue to a dialogue. Right at the beginning of the reading, I say that there will be things I will want to say to my client, but that there will also be other things I will need to check out with him or her. In other words, accurate interpretation depends a lot on context. The other risk of doing too much talking yourself is that you can actually make it difficult for your client to speak out and you could miss valuable pointers as to what is really important.

SHUFFLING AND DEALING

As I talk to my client at the beginning of the session I shuffle the cards. I then ask the client to shuffle them and explain that the important thing is for him or her to handle the cards and then to hand them back when he or she feels ready. I ask my client not to talk as he or she shuffles, but don't over-concern myself with asking the client to think about questions.

Some Tarot readers shuffle the cards and then ask the client to cut the pack, others deal straight from the top of the pack once the client has shuffled, but I prefer a different system. When the pack is handed back to me, I fan the cards out on the silk cloth, face down, and ask the client to choose ten and to lay them, face down, on top of each other. I feel that this invites more involvement from the client and helps to strengthen the bond between you, your client, and the cards. This also means that the first card chosen is the last card to be laid, the important outcome card.

I always count silently as the client chooses the cards, as a person is often so engaged in selecting that he or she makes a mistake. I also note the way in which the cards are chosen as this offers insights. Some people choose slowly, which is associated with earth/water types, while others choose quickly and immediately, which is associated with fire/air types.

I pick up the undealt cards and hold them as I start to read. Starting with the Celtic Cross I always go to the two past cards first. This is called retrodiction as opposed to prediction and is a useful exercise for inviting the client into the world of symbolism.

Dropped Cards

I always make sure to note any cards that are dropped while the client is shuffling, either memorizing them or placing them to one side of the silk cloth. This relates to the underlying principle that what is important will show and be seen. Sometimes a card will appear to jump out of the pack.

Reversed cards

Once my client has chosen ten cards I sweep up the rest of the pack and put it to one side while I lay out the traditional Celtic Cross spread, turning the cards upward as I go. Not all Tarot readers observe the practice of using reversed cards, a practice that gives the card the opposite meaning. For example, an upright Three of Cups would be joy and celebration, whereas reversed it would signal gloom and unhappiness. I personally have never found that reversed cards "speak" to me, that they do not increase the effectiveness of the reading. Instead, I have found that a positive card can be negated or complicated if it is sandwiched between difficult cards. In the Celtic Cross it is often the card crossing the center card that will reveal a key issue or problem.

INTERPRETING THE CARDS

One of the joys of the Tarot is that it is so visual and immediate, unlike astrology, which looks like a mass of meaningless hieroglyphics to the uninitiated. With a Tarot card you can start by describing the picture, which leads naturally into conveying its meaning.

Take the picture on the Judgement card, for example, with the figures arising from their coffins with outstretched arms. This is so clearly a card of rebirth, a coming back to life, which leads to the theme of fresh starts and new beginnings. It is obvious that you are not making this meaning up.

I have also found that the more sense you can make of the past cards, the more sense you will make of this first spread as a whole. However, it is important not to be disheartened if you draw a blank. If this happens I simply move on, saying that we can come back to the past cards once we have looked at the rest of the spread. Often a story will emerge that will give you a whole new angle and you will be able to integrate the past cards as you go on.

I then concentrate on the center card and the card crossing it. Invariably, the combination of these two cards speaks of where the client is at the present moment, the nature of his or her greatest concern, what is uppermost in the person's mind, and what is in the way. The rest of the cards speak of what is to come and mark out the sequence of events that will lead to the outcome, but I will describe the significance of each card position in more detail later when we look at the merits and meanings of the various spreads.

QUESTIONS TO AVOID
In the example readings given for the Major Arcana cards I mention a couple of issues that I refuse to deal with. The most obvious are questions about death, and I discuss this in direct relation to the Death

Third party questions
I try to avoid "third party" questions—questions about other people when there is no direct link between them and my client's own concerns. Often such questions are vague and concern siblings or children, such as "What's happening in my sister's life?" I usually point out that this is his or her reading, not the sister's, and that she herself would need to put her own questions forward. However, I would take on any question that is specific as long as it is asked with real love and concern, such as "Will my sister get the new job she's applied for?"

card, card 13. I wholeheartedly believe that it is unethical to try and answer such questions, if only because you might get it wrong. Tarot or astrological readings are there to help us deal with life—practically, mentally, and spiritually—and not to tell us when we, or anyone else, are due to shuffle off our mortal coil.

In relation to the Empress, card 3, I discuss avoiding the question, "Will I ever have a child?" In fact, I try to avoid any question that begins with "Will I ever?" as it generally lacks context, providing no framework for divination. Also, these kinds of questions often relate to something very deeply desired, such as "Will I ever get married?" A negative answer to a question of longing or even desperation can be devastating and do a lot of damage. A good way of discouraging a client from this line of questioning is to remind him or her that a Tarot reading is really about the present moment and the coming six months or so, and not about events in the distant future.

SAYING WHAT YOU SEE

Sometimes in a reading I can be in full flow and then suddenly find that a word, a phrase, or even a whole sentence is echoing in my head. Some may call this being psychic, some may call it intuition. I think that it is partly due to finding yourself in an intense, one-to-one situation, in which your energy is completely focused. If you are working effectively, you will be in a highly receptive, tuned-in state, which creates heightened feelings and increased levels of awareness. Sometimes the words seem unrelated to

The card underneath shows your present position, where you are now. The card on top, one of the most important cards in the spread, shows what crosses you or is causing problems.

The Empress often occurs in the context of motherhood, pregnancy, or an imminent or recent birth. In terms of relationships, it indicates that our love is healthy rather than an obsession or a mistake.

The Death card rarely signifies actual death. Symbolically it tells us that something is "dead," or ending, whether it is a situation, way of life, job, or relationship. The changes symbolized are usually deep and permanent.

the reading, odd, or even ridiculous, but I have learned to pay attention to them and to say them anyway. Sometimes your client will make immediate sense of what you are saying, sometimes not, in which case I simply ask that he or she store it away as it may make sense at a later date.

SAYING WHAT YOU SEE WHEN THE ANSWER IS "NO"

I have already referred to the problem of being a "good news" Tarot reader. In other words, we hope and desire to say what the client wants to hear and it is never easy to say what he or she doesn't want to hear. This is another reason why I find it difficult to do readings for people I already know, as the desire to come up with the "right" answers is even stronger.

There are two important points to bear in mind. Firstly, we are not doing anyone any favors if we gloss over difficulties or glamorize the more difficult cards. I still remember vividly when this happened to me, many years ago before I started reading the Tarot myself. I was in a difficult relationship but totally infatuated with the man and desperate for it to work out. The upshot of the reading was that he was crazy about me, that we were meant to be together and that it would all work out wonderfully well. It didn't. All that happened was that my already blind faith was strengthened and I carried on ignoring all the obvious problems.

Secondly, people want their problems or issues to be validated. If someone is already unhappy, in trouble, in debt, and so on, the last thing he or she wants to hear is that everything in the garden is rosy when he or she knows only too well that it isn't. We have to remember that we

Cards repeating

Once I have finished with the Celtic Cross spread I will then lay other spreads for more specific questions, if necessary. If I am going to do another spread, I sweep up the ten cards on the table and place them at the back of the pack, which has not been shuffled since my client originally handed it back to me. I ask them to shuffle again and I go through the same procedure, fanning the cards out face down and asking my client to choose as many cards as is necessary. At this point it is important to notice if one or more cards from the first spread reappear, and it is amazing how often this happens. Just as with dropped cards, repeated cards help you to see what is important, that which needs to surface, and often a repeat card will act as a confirmation or as a "testimony" to an interpretation.

are being consulted to provide insights and answers, not platitudes.

The flip side of the coin is that we don't have to be gloom and doom merchants either. Even with the most difficult spreads it is often a case of exploring a situation in order to find the best way forward, to find ideas and coping strategies, rather than delivering finite judgments. When it does finally come down, however, to denying someone's wish, all we can do is to let that person down as gently as possible. I usually say things such as, "Well, I know that this isn't exactly what you want to hear, but I have to tell you what I see—and the truth is that the picture isn't terribly encouraging." Or, "I hate to burst your bubble, but it doesn't look as if this is going to work out in exactly the way you would like." Or, "I wish I could tell you that this is going to work out perfectly but, unfortunately, I don't think that is likely."

In extreme cases, if someone seems hell bent on a path of personal disaster for whatever reason, I would be more urgent and emphatic, saying something like, "If you really are determined to pursue this, then you must be prepared for a tough battle." Or, "This really isn't the easiest of pictures and maybe you need to ask if you're setting yourself up for a lot more trouble." And so on.

HOW TO FINISH

Getting started can be difficult but drawing the reading to a satisfactory close is just as important. Firstly, you can make it a lot easier if you have been clear in advance as to the length of the consultation. Whenever someone makes an appointment I always say that they can expect to be with me for between 30–45 minutes, depending on how much there is to talk about, and I always have a small clock on my table. This is a reminder of the framework of time but it also means that you don't have to keep looking at your watch, which can be off-putting or offensive. I have found that most people will draw the reading to a natural close with you as the time to finish approaches.

However, if a client who seems unaware of the passage of time, it is a case of finding a way to gently wind things up. If I sense early enough that the time-keeping has gone adrift, I anticipate the close with, "Well, we've got another five/ten minutes left. Is there anything else you'd like to ask about, anything in particular you'd like to focus on?" I then end by summarizing the main points of the reading and ask what has been the most interesting or valuable part of the reading for him or her.

Timekeeping
You will inevitably have the experience of a client who seems settled in for the next few hours, oblivious to the clock. This mostly happens with someone who is fascinated by the Tarot. If there are real issues that genuinely merit further work, then I suggest a follow-up appointment.

READING **SPREADS**

As the Tarot has grown in popularity, so has the number of different spreads you can lay. There are no hard and fast rules about which spreads you should use and it is a case of experimenting and finding out the ones that work best for you.

The first thing I do when I start laying out a spread, and before I say a word, is to absorb the overall feel of the reading. Most spreads present rather mixed pictures, but your first impressions and gut reactions can be extremely helpful. The Tarot is so visual that your first impression may be something very simple, such as light or dark, easy or difficult, happy or sad. The general picture can be just as important as the individual cards and paying attention to this helps to keep the reading fluid.

FIRST CONSIDERATIONS

At a more conscious or systematic level you can note if there is a dominance of any particular group and, again, keep it simple. I also note which are the most difficult cards of the spread and where they sit. If they are in the past, then the worst is over, if they are in the future, then there are problems ahead that will need to be worked through. If the outcome card is positive, then doing battle with these problems should prove worthwhile. If it is negative, the chances are that you are fighting a losing battle.

This overall assessment provides a framework for the reading, an "at-a-glance" interpretation, and is very quick to do. If you practice, you will find that it is all in your head by the time you lay the last card, and you will need no more than a moment or two before starting the reading.

On that point, I find that deliberating for too long before starting to speak is counter-productive. I become hesitant and the client gets nervous. I try to jump straight in, usually by starting with the past cards or sometimes with the present moment. The information that comes from you at this point, and the feedback you receive, will add to the framework of the whole reading, as it is through these cards that you will establish the context of your client's life and questions.

Keep it simple

I have found that long-winded, complicated spreads are ineffective. They can be difficult to learn and certain designated meanings can seem rather pointless. There are hundreds of spreads to choose from, but I tend to stick to the ones presented in this chapter, as they are perfectly adequate for covering any kind of question.

As you lay out a spread and before you start to speak, it is important to get an overall feel of the reading. Your first impressions can be extremely helpful.

If there are more than three or four cards from the Major Arcana, and especially if they hold important positions, you can expect to see major events and life changes.

A proliferation of any of the Minor Arcana groups will direct you to matters pertaining to that suit, such as money matters for the Pentacles.

A dominance of the Court cards often shows the presence, influence, or interference of other people in your life.

THE **CELTIC CROSS** SPREAD

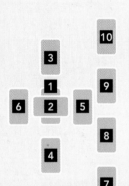

By far the most commonly used spread, and the one with which I start all of my readings, is the Celtic Cross. Depending on which book you consult, you will find slight variations in terms of the order of the cards and their designated meanings.

I present the Celtic Cross here as I first learned it, from Juliet Sharman-Burke's *The Complete Book of Tarot*. [18] The cards are numbered in the order in which they are laid. As well as the traditional meanings, for example, "What is beneath you—passing out of your life," I also use the points shown opposite. In addition, I use my own timing measures, assigning the current month to cards 1 and 2, and adding one month each to card 3 and cards 6–10. This means that the outcome card relates to no more than six months ahead. This is not rigid, but a guideline.

THE CELTIC CROSS SPREAD

1 Present position
2 What crosses you
3 What is above you—future
4 What is beneath you—passing out of your life
5 What is behind you—the past
6 What is before you—the future
7 Where you will find yourself
8 Your surroundings and/or how others see you
9 Your hopes or fears
10 The outcome

The numbering below reflects the order in which the cards are interpreted.

4 What is beneath you—passing out of your life

I always start by interpreting the past cards, which refer to a slightly longer time scale. This card relates to the point that is furthest away in the past and generally speaks of events that have occurred no less than 12 months ago. On some occasions you will find that it speaks of events further back in time. The importance of this card should not be underestimated, as that which is passing out of your life has left its mark, directly or indirectly, in shaping the present.

5 What is behind you—the past

This card generally relates to the recent past, to events of the last six months or so. Again, this is not rigid, but a guideline. I frequently find that the combination of cards 4 and 5 describes a turning point, or a sequence of events or choices that have influenced or changed you and that largely account for where you are in the present moment.

1 Present position

This card describes where you find yourself in the here and now. This may speak either of your outer world, such as a key experience currently unfolding, or of your inner world, such as your emotional state or attitude. It also can be a combination of the two.

2 What crosses you

This is one of the most important cards in the spread. It nearly always points to the heart of the matter—the thing or person who is causing you problems or getting in the way of what you really want. More often than not the combination of cards 1 and 2 will sum up your current predicament.

3 What is above you—future

This card speaks of issues arising—what is to come in the very near future. Generally I find that this relates to the month ahead.

6 What is before you—the future

This card also relates to the near future, generally to no more than two months ahead. Very often cards 3 and 6 work together to show imminent events or influences.

7 Where you will find yourself

This card speaks mostly of your emotional state, whether you will find yourself in a positive or negative place in relation to another person or to a specific issue.

8 Your surroundings and/or how others see you

This card speaks of your environment and what is going on around you. It can also illustrate the image you project, consciously or unconsciously.

9 Your hopes or fears

This card relates to your special wishes or to the thing that you are most worried about.

10 The outcome

The outcome card in any spread is always one of the most important cards as it speaks of the end of the matter, the final result.

I should add that I do not always use these specific categories for the last four cards. In addition to the traditional meanings, I find that cards 7–10 tend to show the sequence of events to come as well as your feelings, wishes, and environment. Designated meanings are there to assist, not restrict, our interpretation and it is important to stay flexible.

THE **RELATIONSHIP** SPREAD

You won't be surprised to learn that this I use this spread all the time. Questions about love, relationships, and affairs of the heart are by far the most common questions that readers are asked.

The Relationship spread is extremely simple, but it can provide a wealth of information, either for someone who is already involved in a relationship or for someone who is hoping to meet someone new. You can also use this spread for family or business relationships.

The spread consists of seven cards, one for the person asking the question (the querent) and another for the partner. These two cards are laid first and the other five are laid above them in the shape of a crescent or horseshoe.

The other cards address, in turn, the current situation, issues arising, the heart of the matter, the short-term future, and the long-term future.

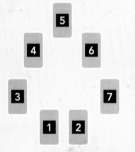

THE RELATIONSHIP SPREAD

1 The querent
2 The partner
3 Current situation
4 Issues arising
5 Heart of the matter
6 Short-term future
7 Long-term future

1 The querent

This card acts as the significator for the person asking the question. It shows how he or she feels about the relationship and how he or she stands in relation to his or her partner.

2 The partner

This card acts as the significator for the person about whom the question is being asked. It shows how he or she feels about the relationship and his or her attitude to the querent.

3 Current situation

This card shows the nature of the relationship in its present form. If there are problems in a relationship, this card can sum up the key issues and the current mood.

4 Issues arising

This card shows the immediate future of the relationship, where it is heading, and the nature of any important issues between the two people.

5 Heart of the matter

This card can act as a lynchpin for the reading. A positive card indicates that the prospects are good even if there are difficulties to be worked at.

6 Short-term future

I assign this card to the ensuing six to twelve months. A positive card indicates that the relationship is headed in the right direction. A difficult card shows problems looming. However, it would only spell the end of the relationship or show that a new love interest is a non-starter if the final card is also negative.

7 Long-term future

I assign this card to the following year. A difficult card does not bode well for the future, as it indicates either that the relationship will be a struggle or that it won't stand the test of time. A positive card promises a happy outcome. Even if the rest of the cards show difficulties, it can indicate that the relationship is worth working at.

Will he ask me to marry him?

When the positive Cups cards appear in any question about a relationship, this is an indication of success and happiness. In this reading the querent is shown by the Nine of Cups—contentment—and even better, her partner is shown by the Knight of Cups, the suitor, so I could safely say that a proposal was imminent. The way ahead also looked rosy with the Queen of Wands showing the current situation—confident and settled—and the two following Major Arcana cards showing progress and completion. The immediate future card of the Two of Wands spoke of planning ahead, and the excellent outcome card, the Six of Wands, promised success.

THE **HORSESHOE** SPREAD

This is a very easy and useful spread that can be used to answer a vast range of questions.

I use this as a second spread after the Celtic Cross for any specific question that does not concern relationships. As you can see, this spread is almost identical to the one used for relationships, comprising of the same crescent of five cards but without the two cards beneath.

THE HORSESHOE SPREAD
1 **Current situation**
2 **What is before you**
3 **Heart of the matter**
4 **Short-term future**
5 **Long-term future**

1 Current situation
This card shows the present state of affairs, the querent's attitude or state of mind, or a combination of both.

2 What is before you
This card shows the immediate future of the matter, issues arising, and the first major stepping stone in the way ahead.

3 Heart of the matter
As with the relationship spread, this card holds the center position, giving it great weight in terms of the overall picture. It can reveal the key issues—the matters around which everything else will revolve. If this card indicates another person, this could be someone who holds some power in the situation, or whose actions or decisions will be pivotal.

4 Short-term future
The first outcome card indicates how events will take shape over the next six months. A positive card shows that you are on the right track. A difficult card indicates that results will be hard won, but the long-term future card will have the final say.

5 Long-term future
The final outcome card is crucial. A difficult card generally indicates failure, that the matter will either come to nothing or end badly. A positive card indicates that we will get the results that we want. If the rest of the spread is mostly positive, then we can expect results swiftly. If it is mostly difficult, then we will get what we want eventually, but not without considerable effort.

OTHER **SPREADS**

ONE-CARD READING

This is not something I use very often, but if you get a clear-cut question that just requires a "yes" or "no," this can be a quick and effective way of answering it. You could, of course, reduce most questions to a simple "yes" or "no" answer, but you would then miss out on the exploration of other influences or factors playing a part in the bigger picture. You will find an example of a one-card reading for the Page of Cups, on page 117.

THREE-CARD READING

This is a very simple but effective spread. I tend to use it when a question is straightforward and clear-cut. The designated meanings are the past influences and main issues, the current state of affairs, and how the situation will turn out in the end.

A 3-CARD READING
1. **Immediate past**
2. **Present**
3. **Future**

Devising your own spreads

As you learn to use the Tarot and how to become an effective reader, it is easier to stick with a couple of traditional spreads. As you become more proficient, there is nothing to stop you from devising your own ways of reading the cards. The golden rule is consistency.

If you devise your own spread and assign a specific card to the present moment, or a specific card to describe the querent, these cards should keep those meanings every time you lay this particular spread. As noted after the Celtic Cross spread, some flexibility is an asset

to the art of interpretation, but it is important to start off with a firm framework. Past cards should always relate to the past and future cards to the future. Suddenly deciding to swap meanings around will result in divinatory chaos.

The most important thing is to learn a repetoire of spreads that you feel comfortable with and that give you enough scope to tackle a range of questions. As a general rule, the spreads you like, and that you find the easiest to do, will be the ones that work the most powerfully for you.

INDEX

FOOTNOTES

1   *The Shorter Oxford English Dictionary*, London, Guild Publishing, 1990

2   Jung, Carl. *Man and His Symbols*, London, Aldus Books, 1964, p. 41

3   Jung p.41

4   Hyde, Maggie. *Jung and Astrology*, London, The Aquarian Press, 1992, p. 69

5   Jung p.41

6   Greene, Liz. *The Astrology of Fate*, London, Unwin Paperbacks, 1984

7   Fontana, David. *The Secret Language of Symbols*, London, Pavilion Books, 1993,p. 171

8   Ozaniec, Naomi. *The Element Tarot Handbook*, Shaftesbury, Dorset, Element Books, 1994, pp. 31-32

9   Greene, Liz. p. 10

10   Casey, Caroline W. *Making the Gods Work for You*, New York, Three Rivers Press, 1998, p. 106

11   Casey, Caroline p.106.

12   Gibran, Kahlil. *The Prophet*, London, Heinemann, 1989, p. 93

13   *The Shorter Oxford English Dictionary*

14   Pollack, Rachel. *78 Degrees of Wisdom*, London, Thorsons, 1995, p. 98

15   Pollack, Rachel. p.98

16   Congreve, William. "The Mourning Bride," from *A Dictionary of Famous Quotations*, Pan Books, London, 1973

17   Walker, Barbara G. *The Woman's Dictionary of Symbols and Sacred Objects*, San Francisco, HarperSanFrancisco, 1998, p. 134

18   Sharman-Burke, Juliet. *The Complete Book of Tarot*, Pan Books, London, 1985

ACKNOWLEDGMENTS

A gigantic thank you to the following people. It's the old cliché, but without them this book would never have happened.

To two awesome and extraordinary earth women, both with lucky Jupiter in powerful Scorpio conjunct my Ascendant. Therapist extraordinaire Capricorn Jocelyn Chaplin—you changed my life when you showed me that "weird" was "unusual," and revealed to me my own power to create. And my agent, the amazing Taurean Annie Tatham Mannall—you turned the tide, as only you know, and materialized my dream.

To all my colleagues—Elisabeth Brooke, for your practical support, encouragement, and insights, especially in the early days of ideas and trial runs. For years of inspiration, everyone at the Company of Astrologers, notably Maggie Hyde, Geoffrey Cornelius, Sally Kirkman, Pat Blackett, Vernon Wells, Graeme Tobyn, Alan Jones, and the late great Derek Appleby.

To friend and therapist Paul Hitchings, for years of love, support, encouragement, and countless hours of fascinating discussion and debate.

To Alice and Pete Hatch, whose friendship and support have been so much appreciated throughout.

Grateful thanks to all my clients who generously allowed their readings to be used.

To the team at Carroll and Brown for your collective brilliance, expertise, and faith in this book.

Last but of course by no means least, to my "earth partner" Charles ♥, for your love but especially for your incomparable enthusiasm, and to my twin sister Sue, to whom this book is dedicated, who just never stops believing in me.

Carroll & Brown would also like to thank:
Additional editorial and design assistance
Stuart Moorhouse, Jim Cheatle, Tom Broder
Production Karol Davies, Nigel Reed
Photographer Jules Selmes
Photographic assistant David Yems
Computer management Paul Stradling
Picture researcher Mirco De Cet
Indexer Hilary Bird

PICTURE CREDITS

Axiom/Steve J. Benbow: 28; 30bl.
CORBIS: 18 Thomas Schweitzer; 51 David Samuel Robbins; 69 Scott Faulkner;
   72 Peter Barrett; 81 Matthew Allan; 88 Phil Banks; 115 Bud Freund;
   130; 133 Tracy Kahn.
Getty Images: 38; 63; 65; 78; 94; 107.
Imagestate: 97; 120.
Sopexa: 84
The White Company: 10; 15 www.thewhiteco.com